The Ultimate Scene Study Series
for Teens Volume II

55 Short Scenes

A Smith and Kraus Book
Published by Smith and Kraus, Inc.
177 Lyme Road, Hanover, NH 03755
smithandkraus.com

First Edition: February 2004
Manufactured in the United States of America
9 8 7 6 5 4 3 2 1

Cover and text design by Julia Gignoux, Freedom Hill Design

Library of Congress Cataloging-in-Publication Data
Lamedman, Debbie.
55 short scenes / Debbie Lamedman.-- 1st ed.
p. cm. -- (The ultimate scene study series for teens ; v. 2) (Young actors series)
ISBN-10 1-57525-338-0 / ISBN-13 978-1-57525-338-1
1. Acting. 2. Young adult drama, American. 3. Teenagers--Drama. I. Title: Fifty-
five short scenes. II. Title. III. Series. IV. Young actor series.
PN2080.L34 2004
812'.6--dc22
2004041747

The Ultimate
Scene Study Series
for Teens
VOLUME II

· · ·

55 Short Scenes

Debbie Lamedman

YOUNG ACTORS SERIES

A Smith and Kraus Book

THE ULTIMATE AUDITION BOOK FOR TEENS SERIES

The Ultimate Audition Book for Teens Volume 1: 111 One-Minute Monologues

The Ultimate Audition Book for Teens Volume 2: 111 One-Minute Monologues

The Ultimate Audition Book for Teens Volume 3: 111 One-Minute Monologues

The Ultimate Audition Book for Teens Volume 4: 111 One-Minute Monologues

The Ultimate Audition Book for Teens Volume 5: 111 Shakespeare Monologues

The Ultimate Audition Book for Teens Volume 6: 111 One-Minute Monologues for Teens by Teens

The Ultimate Audition Book for Teens Volume 7: 111 Monologues from Classical Theater, 2 Minutes and Under

The Ultimate Audition Book for Teens Volume 9: 111 Monologues from Contemporary Literature, 2 Minutes and Under

The Ultimate Audition Book for Teens Volume 10: 111 One-Minute Monologues for Teens by Teens

The Ultimate Audition Book for Teens Volume 11: 111 One-Minute Monologues — Just Comedy!

The Ultimate Audition Book for Teens Volume 12: 111 One-Minute Monologues — Active Voices

THE ULTIMATE SCENE STUDY SERIES FOR TEENS

The Ultimate Scene Study Series for Teens Volume 1: 60 Shakespeare Scenes

THE ULTIMATE MONOLOGUE SERIES FOR MIDDLE SCHOOL ACTORS

The Ultimate Monologue Book for Middle School Actors Volume 1: 111 One-Minute Monologues by Kristen Dabrowski

The Ultimate Monologue Book for Middle School Actors Volume 3: 111 One-Minute Monologues by L. E. McCullough

The Ultimate Monologue Book for Middle School Actors Volume 4: 111 One-Minute Monologues — The Rich, The Famous, The Historical by Kristen Dabrowski

To order call toll-free (888) 282-2881
for more information visit us online at www.smithandkraus.com

CONTENTS

Acknowledgments

Let me begin by thanking my mother, Annette Lamedman. Her patience, support, and overall optimism have helped me get through some low points and I am eternally grateful. My mother is an extraordinary person and I am thankful for all she has given me.

To Marla and McCurtis Kelley, thanks for showering me with support and love and always believing in my efforts.

To Jordan, Max, and Samantha Kelley, thank you for the brainstorming sessions at Sharky's! My wonderful nephews and amazing niece came up with some excellent ideas that truly helped to inspire many of the scenes in this book. I cannot express the overall love and pride these three fill me with each and every day.

To Andy Lamedman and Paula Feig, thanks for your ideas, advice, and your constant support and love.

To Peter Grego, a mentor extraordinaire, I feel privileged to have your words and ideas a part of this book. So many of the concepts of acting that I learned from you, I carry with me each and every day and pass them on to my own students. Thank you for all you have given me.

To Janee Hull-Page, Megan Starr-Levitt, and Lee Isenberg, thanks for reading unedited portions of this book and offering wonderful comments and feedback. I would like to also thank Janee for giving me the motivation to write scenes for multiple characters. Those scenes would not have been written without her terrific suggestion!

To David Green and the gang at CCA, thanks for allowing me the opportunity to do what I do in such a warm and nurturing environment.

To Eric Kraus and Marisa Smith for taking a chance with an unknown writer and continuing to believe in my abilities, I extend my deepest gratitude.

And finally, to my students, who help to stimulate my imagination and make me strive to work harder and be a better person, a better teacher, and a better actor. This book would not have existed without all of you, and I thank you all from the bottom of my heart.

Nic Adams	Corinne AndersonSchoepe	Jessica Bunge
Kirsten Erickson	Kayley FitzMaurice	Lisa Forrest
Tyler Gilbert	Kimmi Jenkins	Destiny Lofton
Sydney Matthews	Kendall Mauvezin	Lauren McClain
Kristen Mitchell	Ashley Melbourne	Natasha Niezgoda
Allison Pounds	Yasmin Rawji	Kensie Sanchez
Trevor Schwerin	Joey Sinko	Jenny Stumpf
Samantha Whitford		

Foreword

I firmly believe that most of us live our lives as a reaction to the stings we received as children and teens. I've never recovered from the fact that Robert Detwieler was cast as the title character in my second grade production of *The Ugly Duckling* and I wasn't! No matter that years later I realized that a tall, overweight, seven-year-old wasn't exactly perfect casting. In some way, though, I am certain this figured into my career choice as a director. So I suppose my ability to channel disappointment into something positive helped me to forgive Sister Francis Mary for her casting blunder. Years later I was auditioning teenagers for admittance to a state-funded summer program. What surprised me was that those with the most theater experience were actually the most "dishonest" actors. I couldn't get some of them to even tell me their names without "acting." What was wrong with this picture?

In the performing arts it is very unlikely that a professional dancer or musician would choose that career path without many youthful years of training. An actor, however, can succeed professionally even if she began her artistic journey in her late teens or adulthood. Maybe part of the answer to bridging these diverse groups and providing a strong foundation can be found in *appropriate dramatic material*. Hence, the importance of Debbie Lamedman's wonderful book! No ducks, princes, or princesses here! No stretching to be a limping, introverted, failed stenographer! No dialects that force the student to hide beneath a cloak of artificiality masking individual personalities and strengths. No! Here instead are scenes that range from the serious to the comedic and that are grounded in experiences with which the student actors are familiar. Here the actors have clearly defined tasks or objectives written in a vernacular they use daily. Here they can tell their truths from their individual perspectives.

Debbie has tested this material on diverse groups of teenagers — and we reap the benefits when we read and produce the scenes. And so will the actors! She has grouped the scenes in the traditional pairings, but notice how even the character names suggest a breadth of diverse casting possibilities. This is very strong material for a changing American populace of the twenty-first century. Students will be thrilled to be cast in any of the pieces.

I preach to my graduate students entering the teaching profession — don't start with a play! Allow the students to find their own voices. Debbie has provided a positive link *and* the voices I've been seeking.

Peter Grego
Coordinator and Professor of Acting and Directing
California State University, Northridge

Introduction

A hhhh . . . scene work. Every young actor I've ever known cannot wait to cast aside the acting exercises and improvisational games and sink his or her teeth into a nice juicy role. I've seen it happen time and time again with my own students. And when I say juicy, I mean juicy! Sixteen-year-old girls longing to play Lady Macbeth. Fifteen-year-old boys begging for a chance to scream "Stellaaaaaa" and let out their inner Stanley Kowalski! But I liken the young actor jumping into roles of this nature to the novice runner, who has yet to step into a proper pair of running shoes; however, he is already planning on finishing that 26.2-mile marathon. Remember, Rome wasn't built in a day!

Sometimes acting isn't acting at all — it's bringing yourself to a role. I wanted to construct scenes that would allow teen actors to create characters they could relate to, circumstances that were similar to situations they had experienced within their own lives — basically a point of reference, a jumping-off place.

The process of creating these scenes started with my own high school acting students. They started off by doing improvisations. Later I built on the scenarios they had developed in the improvs and wrote the actual dialogue for the scenes. I held brainstorming sessions where some of the students were quite forthcoming in letting me know what was happening in their lives. It was a definite collaboration between the actors and myself, and this was extremely helpful since it enabled me to get inside the heads of today's teen. Life is so much more complicated these days, and teens are constantly faced with challenges in their everyday lives — more so than ever before. Consequently, I've tried to reflect those challenges in the scenes included in this book. I have done my best to provide demanding situations with complex characters to let teen actors stretch their acting muscles without feeling the need to play characters completely out of their age range.

Since these are original individual scenes and not excerpts from full-length plays, the only information you will have about a particular character is what is written in the text. Actors, be bold! Expand upon those given circumstances and use your imagination to help you create fully fleshed-out three-dimensional human beings. Use these scenes to expand upon your knowledge of breaking down a piece of text, establishing the beats of a scene, and learning to work moment to moment as you develop a rapport with your scene partner.

In many of the scenes, I have deliberately been vague as to the locale or the environment in which they take place. This will allow further creativity from the actors involved in performing these pieces. A scene that takes place in a crowded hallway at school will certainly be played differently from one that takes place in the security and privacy of one's own bedroom. I hope those of you using this book will feel free to change the environment of the individual scenes and find the most appropriate setting for the dialogues written here.

The diversity of the characters and situations in this book should provide teen actors with a great deal of demanding and challenging material. The people in these scenes may look familiar to you. You may recognize them from your own lives — you may recognize yourself. Remember that the actor is the instrument in which the nature of our craft flows. So use yourself. Tell the truth. The classic plays will always be there; one day you will be ready to tackle those incredible roles. But at this stage of the game, you should start with the familiar. As you grow as a person, the maturity level of the roles you play will grow too. That's the best part about being an actor — it's never one size fits all; our options continue to expand and increase as we develop as human beings. Life experience will always make for better, stronger actors.

Debbie Lamedman

Scenes for Two Females

MAKING A CHANGE

KRISTEN and DESTINY are good friends. They are good students and usually take pride in preparing carefully for all their tests and assignments. But DESTINY has been approached by some other girls who have questionable reputations, and she is willing to sacrifice her own achievements to find out what life is like on the "wilder" side, much to the dismay of KRISTEN, who feels she is making a terrible mistake.

KRISTEN: I thought we could stop at the store and grab some munchies and then go back to my house and just cram all night. You can stay over too, if you want, and that way we can study in the morning before class. How does that sound?

DESTINY: I can't.

KRISTEN: What do you mean you can't? We've been talking about this all week. This final is gonna be huge!

DESTINY: I know. But I think I want to study on my own.

KRISTEN: But we always study together. It's so much easier. We always do so well when we study together.

DESTINY: I know. It's just that . . . well . . . the truth is some other kids asked if I would study with them and they sort of need my help . . . so I said OK.

KRISTEN: What kids?

DESTINY: Tricia and Jill.

KRISTEN: Tricia and Jill? They're total stoners!

DESTINY: They're not so bad. They really want my help.

KRISTEN: Well . . . I guess you could tell them to come over my house. We can form a study group.

DESTINY: No, that's OK. I mean, Jill says her house is empty so there won't be any distraction. Full fridge, empty house. It's a perfect combination for a study session.

KRISTEN: *(Hesitantly.)* So, can I come?

DESTINY: *(Uncomfortable.)* I don't know. I mean, they didn't mention anyone else — they just asked me.

KRISTEN: Well, they know we're good friends. And I can help them too. I've always thought they were kind of . . . I don't know . . . weird I guess . . . standoffish — but if you say they're OK then why not?

DESTINY: *(Gently, but a little frustrated with KRISTEN'S pushiness.)* Why not is because they invited me . . . not you.

KRISTEN: Invited? You're just helping them study, right? It's not like you're going to a party.

(DESTINY avoids making eye contact with KRISTEN and doesn't respond.)

KRISTEN: It's a party? You're going to a party? The night before we have one of the biggest finals of our lives? Are you out of your mind?

DESTINY: No Kristen, I think for the first time in my life I'm thinking clearly!

KRISTEN: What are you talking about?

DESTINY: My life is so dull and boring. I'm sick of it. I always do the right thing. I always do what's expected of me. I get good grades and have nice friends, blah, blah, blah . . . So what is the big deal if one time I blow off studying for a test that's not gonna mean anything in ten years from now anyway! I'll probably still do fine on it without studying. And for once, I'll have the chance to have a little fun.

KRISTEN: Your idea of fun is to hang out with Tricia and Jill? And who knows who else from their skanky little clique. They're total potheads, Destiny. Are you gonna start smoking just so you can be cool? Just so you won't be bored anymore? You're crazy! You're gonna blow everything that you've worked so hard to achieve.

DESTINY: Thanks for the lecture, *Mom*. Look Kristen, I don't need you to tell me what to do. I get enough of that at home. Maybe you're just jealous because those girls *didn't* ask you! I guess they just recognize a dweeb when they see one!

KRISTEN: If that's true, then why did they ask you?

DESTINY: Very funny.

KRISTEN: I can't believe you're doing this.

DESTINY: Well it's my decision to make. I don't need your approval to do what I want.

KRISTEN: No, I guess you don't. I've just been your friend since first grade, but obviously you don't need me around anymore . . . now that you've got some newer hipper friends to hang out with.

DESTINY: I just want to do something different for a change. Why can't you understand that? Aren't you bored with the same old thing every day, the same old people, the same conversations? God, sometimes I think I'm gonna lose my mind.

KRISTEN: No Destiny. I'm not bored. I like my life. I like my friends. And if I did decide I wanted to make a change, I wouldn't choose to hang out with a bunch of stoners the night before a very big test. You're making a huge mistake, and I don't care if you're mad at me for saying so.

DESTINY: Fine. You've had your say. You do what you want and I'll do what I think is right for me. And I don't think I'm making a mistake at all. I think I'm smart enough to know what I'm doing.

KRISTEN: Well, I hope you're right. *(Pause.)* So, I guess I'll see you tomorrow. And I guess . . . well . . . have fun, I guess.

DESTINY: I'm sure I will. Things are going to be much better for me from now on. You'll see — I can party all night and still get good grades too. Who says you can't have it all? *(KRISTEN starts walking away and DESTINY calls out after her.)*

DESTINY: *(Good-naturedly.)* Don't stay up too late studying!

KRISTEN: *(Annoyed.)* You've got to be kidding me! Look who's talking about staying up late. I'll be amazed if you show up at all.

DESTINY: I'll be there. And I'll ace it too. Just wait and see.

END OF SCENE

SHATTERED

KIMMI is LAUREN'S older sister. Recently she experienced a terrible tragedy when her boyfriend of one year was killed in a car accident. A beautiful vase that he had given to her for their one-year anniversary, one of the only keepsakes KIMMI had to remember him by, was broken by LAUREN while she was poking around KIMMI'S room — something she wasn't supposed to be doing. LAUREN has just finished cleaning up the shattered remains of the vase when KIMMI enters.

KIMMI: What are you doing in here?

LAUREN: *(Startled.)* Huh? Oh, God you scared me. I didn't hear you come in.

KIMMI: So answer my question. What are you doing in here?

LAUREN: Um . . . nothing.

KIMMI: You're just standing in the middle of my room staring off into space. Do that in your own room, OK? I told you not to come in here.

LAUREN: Right. Sorry. Won't happen again.

(LAUREN starts to leave.)

KIMMI: Wait a minute! *(Looking at her dresser.)* What did you take?

LAUREN: Nothing. I swear.

KIMMI: Something's missing and you're acting weird — or guilty. What did you take?

LAUREN: Kimmi, I didn't take anything. Honest. I was looking for that new lipstick you got the other day. I thought it was a really great color and I wanted to try it. But I couldn't find it so . . . I'm leaving.

KIMMI: *(Realizing what item is missing from her dresser.)* Oh my God — where's my vase? Where's Jason's vase?

LAUREN: Um . . . you probably moved it. Didn't you move it?

KIMMI: Where would I move it to, Lauren? This was the perfect spot for it. I could see it before I went to sleep and it was the first thing I saw when I woke up. I never moved it! *(Walking toward LAUREN threateningly.)* What did you do with it?

LAUREN: Why would you automatically think *I* did something to it?

KIMMI: Because you are the only one who ever comes in here besides me. Everyone else in this family respects my privacy! You're just a little creep who is always causing trouble!

LAUREN: *(Quietly, hurt.)* I just wanted to borrow your lipstick.

KIMMI: I swear to God, Lauren, I'm putting a lock on this door. Stay the hell out! Don't use my lipstick, don't wear my clothes, don't talk on my cell phone — God — get your own life, would you?

LAUREN: I have a life, thank you very much.

KIMMI: Good — go live it and stay out of mine.

LAUREN: *(Begins to leave.)* Fine. *(Muttering under her breath.)* And see if you'll ever get your precious vase back.

KIMMI: What did you say?

LAUREN: Nothing.

KIMMI: What did you say about the vase? You have it, don't you? Why would you be so mean? You know how much it means to me.

LAUREN: I don't have it! And look who's talking about being mean. You treat me like crap. Like I don't even exist. You care more about that dumb old vase and your stupid dead boyfriend than you do about your own living, breathing sister!

KIMMI: *(Moves in toward LAUREN and slaps her across the face.)* Don't ever say anything like that again. How can you possibly understand what I'm feeling? You have no idea what it feels like to lose someone you feel so strongly about. Now, I'm going to ask you one more time . . . and you better tell me the truth . . . what did you do with the vase?

LAUREN: *(Shocked by the slap and extremely upset.)* It was an accident.

KIMMI: *(Working to remain calm.)* What was an accident?

LAUREN: I really was looking for your lipstick. And I was moving stuff around on your dresser to try and find it. And I accidentally bumped the vase and it fell. I was gonna try and glue it together, but it shattered, Kim. There were about a million pieces. So I swept it up and I was hoping you wouldn't notice, but of course you did. I know you don't think I understand, but I *do* know how much you loved Jason. I'm really sorry, Kimmi. It really was an accident.

KIMMI: *(Coldly.)* Get out.

LAUREN: I said I was sorry.

KIMMI: And I said get out.

LAUREN: What do you want me to do? Get down on my knees and beg your forgiveness?

KIMMI: What I want is for you to get . . . out . . . of . . . my . . . ROOM!!

LAUREN: So I guess you're never gonna talk to me again.

KIMMI: That's a very good idea. *(She takes LAUREN by the arm and practically pushes her toward the door.)* Starting now! *(KIMMI sits down and looks around the room. Puts her head in her hands.)*

END OF SCENE

METAMORPHOSIS

MOLLY has feelings for a boy who used to be a nerd, but who has recently transformed into a handsome young man. She's reluctant to talk about her feelings, but she decides to tell her friend ABBY because she can no longer keep it to herself and she needs to talk about it.

MOLLY: I need to tell you something. But you have to swear you won't tell a soul.

ABBY: Who am I gonna tell?

MOLLY: You've been known to blab secrets before.

ABBY: Not if they were really huge secrets. I've only told things that weren't very important.

MOLLY: Well this is huge.

ABBY: Really?

MOLLY: So promise.

ABBY: Yeah. I promise. What is it?

MOLLY: I'm not kidding, Abby. My very reputation is at stake if anyone finds this out.

ABBY: Really? This *is* huge!

MOLLY: So?

ABBY: So? Oh . . . so I promise. I swear. I'll take this to my grave. What's going on?

MOLLY: I think I'm in love.

ABBY: Really? That's fantastic! Oh wait . . . you're not in love with Mr. Freedman, are you? I mean, he's a great-looking teacher and everything, but he's an older man and he could lose his job and possibly go to jail and you could be screwed up for the rest of your life . . . not to mention that he's married and I think I heard that his wife is gonna have a baby so I think you should really . . .

MOLLY: *(Interrupting.)* Would you shut up for a second? God, you have an active imagination!!

ABBY: Well, there's no need to be rude.

MOLLY: Sorry. I'm sorry. But you just got so carried away and . . . it's *not* Mr. Freedman. I know I said I thought he was hot and everything, but I'm not stupid. It's not him.

ABBY: So . . . who is it? Freedman is the only one I can think of who could ruin your reputation. Besides, I didn't even know you had a reputation.

MOLLY: It's high school. We *all* have reputations! I mean, I know I'm not the most popular kid here, but people would definitely notice if I did something extremely stupid and then I'd have to live with it every day of my life and I'd be miserable.

ABBY: What are you gonna do that's extremely stupid?

MOLLY: Fall in love with someone who's not exactly . . . um . . . he's not exactly . . . socially acceptable.

ABBY: I have no idea who you're talking about! Who *is* this guy!

MOLLY: I'm not kidding — you have to swear you won't say a word or I will *not* tell you.

ABBY: We've been through this. I swear, I swear.

MOLLY: I don't think you're taking this seriously enough.

ABBY: *(Exasperated.)* What do you want me to do? Get down on my knees? Put my hand on a Bible? I won't tell anyone Molly; I absolutely, positively, on my honor promise I will not tell another living person as long as I live. Satisfied?

MOLLY: *(Sighs.)* OK. Thanks. I've gotta trust you on this because if I don't tell someone soon, my head's gonna explode.

ABBY: Drum roll please. *(She makes a drum-roll noise.)*

MOLLY: Cut it out . . . this isn't funny. *(ABBY stops.)* I'm totally serious. This whole situation is stressing me out like you wouldn't believe.

ABBY: I can see that.

MOLLY: OK. Here goes. Lately, I can't seem to stop thinking about this certain guy. And I'm not sure why, because I've never even given him the time of day. And if someone were to ask me what I thought of him, I would have said, ya know, geek, weirdo . . . no one I would want to waste my time on. But in the last month or so, I've noticed that he started to change. He's been looking good. *Really* good. And I actually talked to him the other day in Biology and he's smart. And funny. He wasn't weird or creepy at all. And we started talking and I realized, "Oh, my God. I like this guy." But now I don't know what to do because . . . ya know . . . people still look at him and say . . . *freak!* And I know I shouldn't care what other people think, but what can I say . . . I do. I'm shallow.

ABBY: Oh, my God . . . I know who it is. I can't believe it . . . I know who you're talking about.

MOLLY: You do? You know? You think I'm disgusting, right?

ABBY: It's Jeffrey Dreaksle, isn't it? You like Freaksle Dreaksle?

MOLLY: Oh man, here it comes. I think I'm gonna be sick. I knew I shouldn't have told anyone.

ABBY: No way . . . Moll. Don't be upset. I said I wouldn't tell anyone, and I promise I won't. But Moll . . . all the girls have been talking about Dreaksle. The change is nothing short of miraculous. We can't figure it out. He's totally hot! And we're trying to figure out when this actually happened. It just kinda crept up on all of us, ya know. I mean, he should be in the *Guinness Book of Records* or something, because he went through this . . . what do you call it? A major change? Like a caterpillar into a butterfly? What do you call that again?

MOLLY: Metamorphosis.

ABBY: Right! Damn — shoulda knew that one. Anyway . . . he's a babe. And no one is gonna think you're weird for liking him. I think you should go for it before anyone else makes their move.

MOLLY: Really? Other girls are thinking of making their move?

ABBY: Any day now.

MOLLY: I had no idea. I better move on this. It is amazing, isn't it? He has become absolutely . . . gorgeous!! He was this weird, trippy little wimp and now . . . oh man . . . !

ABBY: It's true. A frog turned into a prince right before our very eyes. It's unbelievable. I wonder if that's ever gonna happen to me? I wouldn't mind going through a meta . . . whatever you call it.

MOLLY: You don't need to go through one — you're fine the way you are.

ABBY: Thanks. But what are you doing still standing here? Girls are flocking as we speak! Now go get 'im!

END OF SCENE

THE SOAP OPERA

GWEN has been invited to a party that CASSIE has not been invited to. Here, they try to figure out the reason why Val would not invite CASSIE to her party and it all becomes quite complicated.

CASSIE: Nice pants. Are they new?

GWEN: They're cool, huh? I just got them yesterday, but do you think they make me look fat?

CASSIE: Are you kidding? You couldn't look fat even if you stuffed a pillow down the front of your shirt.

GWEN: Ohhhh . . . thanks. I got another pair too — I'm saving those for the party.

CASSIE: The party? What party?

GWEN: Val's party. Saturday night. You're going, right?

CASSIE: How can I go when I wasn't even asked?

GWEN: Oh . . . she'll ask you. She probably hasn't seen you yet. When she sees you I'm sure she'll ask you.

CASSIE: She sees me every day in homeroom *and* we have the same fifth period. She's never mentioned it.

GWEN: Well . . . she probably just forgot, ya know? She has a lot on her mind.

CASSIE: Yeah — she has a *party* on her mind. A party she hasn't invited me to. When did she ask you? Yesterday?

GWEN: Uh . . . no . . . not yesterday.

CASSIE: When then?

(GWEN does not answer.)

CASSIE: When did she ask you Gwen? Just tell me.

(GWEN still hesitates to answer.)

CASSIE: Look, I'm not gonna be mad at *you!*

GWEN: *(Looking embarrassed.)* I got an invitation in the mail.

CASSIE: In the mail? She *sent* you an invitation? Well, now it's just obvious, isn't it?

GWEN: What? What's obvious? Maybe she doesn't have your address. Maybe she really did forget.

CASSIE: Maybe she doesn't have my address? . . . maybe she forgot? . . . *maybe* she doesn't want me to come.

GWEN: I don't think that's it.

CASSIE: Then how can you explain it, Gwen? Ya know Val's been kind of giving me the cold shoulder for a while, now that I think about it. I wondered about it last week when I said hi to her and she kind of brushed me off. Then the other day, I came up behind her and put my hands over her eyes — just foolin' around, ya know? She's like all friendly when she didn't know who it was and when she turned around and saw it was me she goes, "God, Cass, grow up — we're not in third grade anymore." She made me feel like a jerk. I was just kidding around.

GWEN: What did you do after she said that?

CASSIE: Nothing. I walked away. I felt so stupid. I guess lately she and I have been drifting apart, but we still have all the same friends. It wasn't that long ago when we were all at Jen's for a sleepover, remember? Everything seemed fine then. Don't you think?

GWEN: That was a great party — I didn't think anything was wrong, but that sleepover was almost three months ago. You know she had a big fight with Sarah last Thursday. She's not talking to Sarah. Sarah must have told you about it — you guys are so tight.

CASSIE: Sarah didn't say it was a *big* fight. She called it a disagreement. No big deal. I thought it was all straightened out. But I *know* she doesn't know about this party. She would have told me if she were going. This is all so lame!

GWEN: Val's mad at Sarah because Sarah was hitting on Drew at lunch the other day.

CASSIE: Yes, but Sarah told me she apologized to Val and told Val that she wouldn't have flirted with Drew if she had known Val liked him. And she said she wouldn't do it again.

GWEN: I know for a fact she invited Drew to her party and

she doesn't want Sarah there because she thinks Drew likes Sarah.

CASSIE: Oh, my God. This is the dumbest soap opera I've ever heard. Val is *such* a control freak. This still doesn't explain why she didn't invite me. I have nothing to do with Drew.

GWEN: Yeah, but you're close with Sarah. Like you said, Val's totally trying to control the whole situation. Wow . . . this is very complicated.

CASSIE: It's ridiculous. What a drama queen. I wouldn't go to this dumb old party now even if she did ask me. Who else is gonna be there? Do you know?

GWEN: I thought I knew but I guess I don't. I mean, I thought you and Sarah were going. Jen can't go 'cause she's got some family thing. Erin's still grounded and I don't think Jamie was invited either. There's not gonna be anyone there that I'm good friends with. Maybe I won't go.

CASSIE: No! You have to go. At least go so you can wear your new pants and stay long enough to tell me how bad it was.

GWEN: You think it's gonna be a bad party?

CASSIE: I have no idea. Depends on who shows up.

GWEN: Maybe Drew won't even come. Oh man — that would make Val soooo mad.

CASSIE: You want her to be mad?

GWEN: Val's not my most favorite person, ya know. She can be a little hard to take sometimes.

CASSIE: Tell me about it!

GWEN: What are *you* doing Saturday night?

CASSIE: Sarah has to babysit her little brother, so I'm going over there just to hang out and eat and watch movies.

GWEN: That's sounds good. No drama.

CASSIE: Well, you're welcome to join us. I know Sarah won't mind if you come over. But consider what will happen when you don't show up to Val's party.

GWEN: I'll be shunned! She'll shun me!

CASSIE: *(Laughing.)* She totally will. You will definitely get the silent treatment — probably for the rest of your life!

GWEN: Why are we friends with her again? She tells *you* to grow up and then look how she acts.

CASSIE: I know — I told you, she's *lame*. Who cares about her stupid party?

GWEN: Sooooo, you're sure it's OK if I hang with you and Sarah Saturday night?

CASSIE: Of course. Pizza, popcorn, movies with hunky men! Ya can't beat it!

GWEN: OK. I'm in. Can I wear my new pants?

CASSIE: Definitely!

END OF SCENE

ELECTION RESULTS

JENNIFER has run for senior class president and lost. She feels, however, that the wrong person was elected, merely voted in based on popularity rather than merit. Here she confronts her opponent SHERYL to offer her a proposition.

JENNIFER: Hey, Sheryl, can I talk to you for a second?

SHERYL: Yeah, what up?

JENNIFER: I kind of need to ask you something — a favor?

SHERYL: What do you want?

JENNIFER: Well, we all know why you won the election, and it wasn't because of your speech.

SHERYL: What are you talking about? My speech was rockin'!

JENNIFER: *(Mimicking her speech.)* "Fo' shizzle, I'm Sheryl and I sizzle . . . put the vote to the name . . . Word!" *(Sarcastically.)* Very presidential.

SHERYL: Obviously — it won me the election.

JENNIFER: Come on, Sheryl. Do you even want to be class president?

SHERYL: I guess . . . yeah. It'll be cool. Why are you hassling me?

JENNIFER: Look, we all know that this was nothing more than a popularity contest. So congrats to you — you're the most popular girl in school. Now, I think you should step aside, you proved what you wanted to prove, and let the right person be the president.

SHERYL: And I suppose you think you're the right person?

JENNIFER: Yes! I really want this. I've been planning this since my sophomore year. I worked very hard on my speech and I intend to work very hard as student body president. And you're just making a joke of the whole thing. You just wanted votes, but you don't want the job and we both know it.

SHERYL: So you're asking me to quit?

JENNIFER: Yeah . . . I guess I am. I think it's the right thing to do.

SHERYL: No way, girl. I don't quit anything.

JENNIFER: I'm asking you to step aside. You don't even care about it; the only thing you wanted was to win. And you did . . . yippee for you! Now let someone who wants the job, do the job. Me!

SHERYL: My mom says it'll look good on my record; I'm *not* giving it up.

JENNIFER: So what do you plan to do next semester as president? What do you plan to change? How are you gonna make this school better?

SHERYL: I don't know . . . God, don't bother me with all that. I'll figure it out.

JENNIFER: No ideas at all?

SHERYL: *(Laughing.)* Yeah . . . I got some ideas about making our lunch periods longer.

JENNIFER: *(Condescendingly.)* Oh, that's just great. You'll go down in history for that one.

SHERYL: Student body presidents don't make that much of a difference and you know it. Name one thing any of the past presidents have done to change this school. *(Pause.)* See . . . you can't — bake sales, carnivals . . . that's the kind of stuff you plan — it's an easy credit as far as I'm concerned. And hey, obviously the people want me.

JENNIFER: *(Angrily.)* I don't know how you managed to win Sheryl, but I don't think it's fair. I did plan on actually doing things to help change the school for the better. All you're going to do is kick back, plan bake sales, and bask in your popularity. I think if you cared at all, you'd let me have the job.

SHERYL: No one is stopping you from being in student government. Be involved, head all the committees if you want, I don't care. But I won the election and I won it *fairly*. And I *will* be senior class president next year, so you just better get used to the idea.

JENNIFER: I'll never get used to the idea. And one of these days Sheryl you're gonna learn that you can't get by just on looks and personality.

SHERLYL: Well I've been doing just fine so far. Don't be so bitter, Jenn — it's not good for the complexion.

(SHERYL starts to walk away.)

JENNIFER: *(Calling after her.)* I can make your life miserable, ya know. See if I won't.

SHERYL: *(Turning around quickly.)* Just try it — *try* to make my life a living hell. But it won't work and you know why? 'Cause I got friends who watch my back. Lots and lots of friends . . . you know, all those people that voted for me — that like me better than they like you! So I'm not too worried about your threats — I got my posse!

JENNIFER: You are just *evil!*

SHERYL: No. I'm popular. *And* I'm the president. Too bad for you. Ta!

(SHERYL walks away gloating. JENNIFER stands frozen — consumed with anger and frustration.)

END OF SCENE

BEEKEEPER

EMILY tries to do her best to protect her friend AMANDA from being stung by a large bumblebee.

EMILY: Whatever you do . . . don't move!

AMANDA: What are you talking about?

EMILY: Stay perfectly calm and still.

AMANDA: You're freaking me out — what are you *talking* about?

EMILY: There's a very large bee on your shoulder.

AMANDA: Where?

EMILY: On your shoulder.

AMANDA: Where?

EMILY: *(Talking very slowly as if to a small child.)* On . . . your . . . shoulder.

AMANDA: *(Shouting.)* *Where* on my shoulder? Which shoulder?

EMILY: You're starting to get hysterical. You really need to remain calm.

AMANDA: *(Takes a deep breath in an effort to be calm.)* Emily . . . please tell me . . . which shoulder is it on?

EMILY: Your right. I mean your left. My right — your left. *(Shouting.)* Your *left* shoulder.

AMANDA: Why are you yelling at me?

EMILY: Sorry. I don't know what to do. You're supposed to ignore bees and eventually they go away.

AMANDA: Why did I wear this sweater today? You're not supposed to wear bright shirts — they attract bees. It probably thinks I'm a flower.

EMILY: It's a really nice sweater.

AMANDA: Thanks.

EMILY: You're welcome.

AMANDA: Em . . . I'm really allergic to bee stings.

EMILY: I know. So just don't panic. Don't move.

AMANDA: Where is it now?

EMILY: Still there. On your shoulder. It's not really doing anything. Maybe it's trying to get pollen from you.

AMANDA: Sick! I'm being humped by a bee.

EMILY: By like, the *queen* bee.

AMANDA: How do you know it's a queen?

EMILY: It's huge.

AMANDA: Are you serious?

EMILY: I wish I were joking. It's the biggest bee I've ever seen!

AMANDA: *Emily!*

EMILY: I'm sorry, but it's true. It's a big black bumblebee. Wow. That's a tongue twister. Big black bumblebee. Big black bumblebee.

AMANDA: Will you please stop saying tongue twisters and concentrate!

EMILY: Sorry. Um . . . what am I concentrating on?

AMANDA: Getting it off of me!

EMILY: OK. Um . . . I'm gonna swipe it.

AMANDA: With what?

EMILY: With uh . . . with a stick? No, that won't work. Oh! I have a magazine in my backpack. I'll use that. I'll roll it up and swipe it.

AMANDA: And you're really gonna piss it off. And then it'll attack me for sure.

EMILY: Well, what do you suggest? Would you like to continue walking down the street with your pet bee sitting on your shoulder?

AMANDA: That's not funny. I'm starting to get a crick in my neck from not moving.

EMILY: He really likes you.

AMANDA: I thought you said it was the queen?

EMILY: OK . . . sorry! *She* really likes you. She doesn't want to move.

AMANDA: It's not moving?

EMILY: Hasn't for some time now.

AMANDA: Is it alive?

EMILY: *(Taking a closer look.)* Uh . . . I think it is . . . Oh my God . . .

AMANDA: What? What? Is it's stinger out? Is it getting ready to sting me? This is it — I'm gonna die for sure! I'm gonna swell up right before your very eyes and just die. So long Em . . . it's been nice knowing you.
(She squinches her eyes together and becomes very tense in preparation for something awful to happen.)

EMILY: You're a very dramatic person. Has anyone ever told you that?

AMANDA: Oh sure — you can be calm — it's not your life on the line here.

EMILY: Open your eyes, Amanda.

AMANDA: I'd rather keep them closed until it's over.

EMILY: Until what's over?

AMANDA: The pain.

EMILY: There won't be any pain.

AMANDA: *(Opening her eyes.)* There won't?

EMILY: This is what's been on your shoulder the whole time! *(She pulls off a black piece of lint from AMANDA'S sweater.)* You were worried for nothing, see?

AMANDA: *I* was worried? You're the one who told me there was a big black bumblebee on my shirt! You practically gave me a heart attack! If I hadn't gotten stung by the bee, I definitely would have had a heart attack.

EMILY: But it's all good. There's no bee. Just some dryer crap on your sweater. I hate when that happens. You should tell your mom to use fabric softener or something. Keeps the lint off.

AMANDA: Wow, I really freaked out there for a while, huh?

EMILY: I would have done the same thing. Who wants a big black bumblebee attacking them?

AMANDA: Yeah! Who *does want* a big black bumblebee attacking them?

EMILY: See — I told you that was fun to say. Big black bulky balding bumblebee!

AMANDA: Let's go back to my house.

EMILY: How come?

AMANDA: I need to change my shirt. Nothing too bright. Wouldn't want to tempt fate, ya know?

EMILY: Good idea. A big black bulky bumblebee bandage barreling backwards!

(AMANDA rolls her eyes at EMILY as they exit.)

END OF SCENE

MOVING

SHELBY and DAWN brainstorm on ways to keep SHELBY from moving out of state with her family when she is just about to enter her final year of high school.

SHELBY: The landlord came by this morning while I was still sleeping. We've got thirty days to get out because he needs money and he has to sell the house.

DAWN: I don't get it. Why can't your mom just fight to keep the place? I mean, isn't that illegal? He can't just kick you out on the street!

SHELBY: He's giving us notice so I guess it is legal. It's not like he's saying we have to be out by tomorrow. I just wish we could buy it, ya know? We've been renting that house for ten years. My whole life is in that house. I don't want to leave.

DAWN: So that's it? You have to move . . . but it's not like you're leaving town or anything, right? You'll find another place nearby, won't you?

SHELBY: Well that's just it. My mom wants to turn this into an "opportunity." She says we should get a fresh start and go where nobody knows us and start new.

DAWN: Well that's just crazy! What did you say?

SHELBY: I told her that it was the cruelest thing she could possibly do to me. Make me start new in my senior year? It's barbaric. Troy was psyched — he doesn't care whether we stay or go — but me? How could she do this to me?

DAWN: Well it's not definite, right? I mean, she's just talking about it . . .

SHELBY: When my mom gets an idea in her head, she usually goes through with it. She's already got some job leads in Seattle and is planning to go there next weekend to check out a couple of places to live. See? Looks like I'm finishing high school in Seattle. This is the end!

DAWN: She can't do this to you! We'll sign a petition — we won't let you go.

SHELBY: It'll never work.

DAWN: We can try! Shelby, she can't make you leave for senior year. We've got so many plans. What about the annual Halloween Ball? What about prom and graduation? You're never gonna have all that in Seattle. Shelby . . . what about *Steve?* I think he's just about to ask you out!

SHELBY: Stop it! You're making me feel worse than I already do — as if that were possible. I don't know how to get through to her. She's so selfish. She's only thinking of what's good for her life. She figures I'll be leaving for college soon anyway, so what's the big deal? Doesn't matter. Ohhhhh . . . she has *no* clue that this move will ruin me. It will absolutely ruin me! It will scar me for life!

DAWN: We're just going to have to do something because she can't get away with this. What about moving in with your dad?

SHELBY: Not an option — don't even go there.

DAWN: OK. Hey . . . don't you have an aunt or something?

SHELBY: Yeah, but she's not gonna want a teenager to move in with her. She's single. No kids. She doesn't want that kind of responsibility.

DAWN: How do you know unless you ask her? She could be totally cool with it. Besides, it's only for one year.

SHELBY: I guess it wouldn't hurt to ask.

DAWN: I'll go with you — I'll be a character witness.

SHELBY: It isn't a trial, Dawn.

DAWN: No. But you might need help convincing her and I could tell her how much I need you here. How all your friends need you here.

SHELBY: It would be so perfect . . . God, I hadn't even thought of asking Aunt Natalie. She is pretty cool — pretty easygoing. Easier to talk to than Mom.

DAWN: Well what are we waiting for? Let's go over there.

SHELBY: Let me call her first and approach it gently. I don't want to overwhelm her.

DAWN: OK, but ya gotta do it today. I mean, your mom has practically got you packed for Seattle.

SHELBY: What if she says no, Dawn? Or worse, what if Aunt Natalie says yes and Mom says no?

DAWN: To quote my mother, "We'll cross that bridge when we come to it." I already have another idea if Aunt Natalie doesn't come through.

SHELBY: Really? What?

DAWN: Me! You'll move in with me! I think I can convince my mom that it's for a good cause.

SHELBY: Oh God, Dawnie! That would be awesome. We could do all sorts of . . .

DAWN: *(Interrupting.)* Focus! Let's not get overly excited. First things first. Plan A: Aunt Nat. Plan B: Me! But whatever happens, you are *not* moving to Seattle! I'll sue your mother for taking away my best friend.

SHELBY: Wow! Thank you! What would I do without you?

DAWN: Let's *not* find out! Now come on. Let's go sweet-talk your aunt. And then we'll work on your mother!

END OF SCENE

AT THE AUDITION

KAYLEY and ALLISON are sisters who have been pushed into show business by their aggressive mother. KAYLEY actually loves the business and is excited to pursue a theatrical career. ALLISON is fed up with other people telling her how to live her life. Suffering from audition anxiety, she finally snaps and tells KAYLEY how she truly feels. KAYLEY is torn between doing what she wants to do, and showing loyalty to her sister.

As the scene begins, KAYLEY is in the middle of doing a vocal warm-up and looking through her sheet music. ALLISON stands frozen staring in the direction of the audition room. KAYLEY collects her things and approaches ALLISON.

KAYLEY: I'm totally nervous. But I'm totally excited too. I think we have a good chance of getting into this show. Think how excited Mom will be when we tell her we got a national tour! *(Pauses. Looks around at the competition.)* Our voices are as good as any of these other girls.

ALLISON: Your voice maybe — but not mine. I can't believe I let you talk me into this. This isn't some dumb little community theater show. This is big time.

KAYLEY: I know. Mom thinks we're ready. I think we're ready. And you'll do great. I love the way you sing. You have to do this. The world needs to see how talented you are.

ALLISON: Gimme a break!

KAYLEY: I'm serious.

ALLISON: You're out of your mind. *(Pause.)* Look — I don't think I can do this.

KAYLEY: Sure you can.

ALLISON: Let me rephrase: I *don't want to do this!!*

KAYLEY: You're just nervous. So am I — it's normal.

ALLISON: No, I'm not. I mean, yes, I'm nervous — of course

I am. But I also know that I got talked into doing this. Talked into doing something that I really don't want to do. Mom has been pushing me my whole life, even when I've showed no interest. I'm sick of it. I'm sick of having her try to live her life through me. Through us. This is her dream, not mine.

KAYLEY: You really don't want to get into this show?

ALLISON: NO! I sing for fun. I sing for me. I don't want to make it a career.

KAYLEY: You never told me that before.

ALLISON: You never asked. You just assumed I wanted it as much as you did.

KAYLEY: But I thought you said it would be fun . . . to both get parts and actually go on tour together. You seemed really excited about it. So what was that all about?

ALLISON: I thought it would be. But now that we're here and I see all these other people taking it all seriously . . . I mean, this means *everything* to you . . . and to them . . . And I know it's not anything I want to do.

KAYLEY: Well . . . what *do* you want to do?

ALLISON: I don't know. That's just it. I want to find out. Maybe I'll go to college and study archaeology or sociology. Maybe I'll start my own greeting card business. I really don't know what I want to do. The only thing I do know, is that I *don't* want to be an actor or a singer. That's the one thing I'm really clear on.

KAYLEY: *(Obviously hurt and disappointed.)* I just wish you would have told me all of this before. You obviously feel really strongly about all this; I can't believe you never told me. What a waste of time — coming here for nothing!

ALLISON: Why? It's not for nothing — you still want to do it.

KAYLEY: I'm not doing it without you.

ALLISON: Why not? We don't have to do *everything* together, do we?

KAYLEY: No, but . . . what's Mom gonna say?

ALLISON: Who cares? It's your life. And it's my life. You

follow your dream and I'll follow mine, whatever it is. We're two different people Kayley, we don't need to be attached at the hip no matter what Mom says. Now, you really want to be in this show, don't you?

KAYLEY: *(Reluctantly.)* Yeah . . . I really do. It's all I ever think about. I want it *really* bad.

ALLISON: Then go for it, silly! Go in there and sing your heart out! And I'll be out here waiting for you and cheering you on.

KAYLEY: Are you sure? I mean, are you absolutely sure you don't want to audition too?

ALLISON: I've never been more sure of anything in my life. I'll be here for your moral support. And I'll be your number one fan when you become famous.

KAYLEY: I can't believe you don't want to do this.

ALLISON: I can't believe you do.

KAYLEY: Mom's probably going to freak when you tell her that you didn't audition

ALLISON: So what? I don't care. She's just gonna have to accept the fact that only one of her daughters is going to be a star. Now you better go — it's almost your turn. I'll be right here when you come out.

KAYLEY: Thanks, Allie, you're the greatest. *(They hug. KAYLEY starts to leave.)* Whoa . . . I'm feeling really woozy all of sudden. Maybe you're right — we *should* both leave.

ALLISON: Oh no you don't. One daughter bailing out on show biz is quite enough for one day. If we both bailed, Mom would definitely have a cow. Now go! I command you!

KAYLEY: *(Shaky, but determined.)* OK. Here I go. Wish me luck.

ALLISON: *(Holding up her crossed fingers as KAYLEY exits.)* Tons! *(She watches KAYLEY go. She lets out a sigh of relief.)*

END OF SCENE

CASTING SPELLS

LILY seeks out HALEY, a girl that is known to prac-
tice witchcraft. LILY is hoping HALEY can help her
capture the affections of a guy who doesn't even know
she exists by casting a love spell.

LILY: Hi, Haley — I know you and I don't know each other
very well, but I was wondering if you had a minute? I sorta
need to ask you something?

HALEY: Hi! Uh . . . Lily, right?

LILY: Yeah, that's right. Do you have time to talk?

HALEY: Sure. What do you need?

LILY: Well, I heard that you know some stuff about . . . ya
know . . . doing spells and stuff?

HALEY: What about it?

LILY: I heard that you're like a practicing witch or something
like that. Is that true?

HALEY: I don't like to talk about it too much because people
hassle me about it. But yeah — I'm Wiccan.

LILY: And you know how to do spells and stuff?

HALEY: I'm not Sabrina the teenage witch if that's what you're
thinking. It's my belief system. I practice a craft — it's not
just a bunch of hocus-pocus.

LILY: I know — I mean, I *don't* really know, but I respect you
for your beliefs. I was just wondering if you could help me.

HALEY: You're interested in Wicca?

LILY: Well, I'm interested in learning how to do a spell.

HALEY: But it doesn't work like that.

LILY: What do you mean?

HALEY: Well, it's not like in the movies. It's not like whipping
up potions and stuff. It's about spirituality — respecting nature — a path that leads to empowerment.

LILY: Whoa! That's heavy. My mom thinks you guys are dangerous. Like some weird cult.

HALEY: We're not — we're all about respecting the universe. It's a beautiful religion.

LILY: Well all I wanted to know was . . . I was just hoping you had the uh . . . ability . . . to um . . . help me get Erick Von to . . . um . . . to like fall in love with me.

HALEY: Now *that's* dangerous.

LILY: Why? I'm not asking you to do anything evil.

HALEY: But doing magic to control someone else's destiny is dangerous. You need to do spells that will make *you* become a better person. It's not about making someone do something against their will. You have to be careful when you mess around with this stuff.

LILY: I just want him to like me. It would be nice if he even *noticed* me! I didn't realize this witch stuff was so complicated.

HALEY: Look, Lily — there's no such thing as snapping your fingers and having your wish granted. The universe doesn't work like that. But if you start visualizing positive things happening, and sending out positive energy, then good things should come back to you. Basically, that's how it works. But you have to put some effort into it.

LILY: My mom is sooo wrong about you guys. You're totally mellow and everything. You make me feel so relaxed. *And* stupid. I feel so stupid for even coming up to you and asking you such a lame favor.

HALEY: Don't feel stupid. You would never have known if you hadn't asked. And if you're interested in finding out more about Wicca, let me know. But, I won't teach you any spells — it's really not a good idea.

LILY: Have you ever actually done any?

HALEY: *(Seems to be amused at first, but then starts to become annoyed.)* You crack me up! You think it's like that movie *The Craft* where I can fly in on a broomstick and make everyone do whatever I want them to do. It's not like that. And it's hard to explain what it is like — unless you're interested in joining. I take it all very seriously — I feel it's sacred and I don't feel comfortable talking about it with people who look at me like I'm a circus freak.

LILY: Hey . . . I never meant any harm. I'm just totally curious. And you're so cool and mysterious and I've always wanted to know more. But like I said before, I respect your beliefs and I won't bug you about it anymore. I'm sorry — I didn't mean to hurt your feelings.

HALEY: It's cool. Just so you know how I feel.

LILY: A second ago — you said something about joining?

HALEY: Yeah. You interested?

LILY: Joining what exactly?

HALEY: Our community.

LILY: You mean like a coven?

HALEY: Some call it that.

LILY: . . . uh . . . no disrespect, OK . . . but uh . . . that just sort of freaks me out . . . a *coven*? That's just a little too weird for me. Sorry.

HALEY: It's cool. I understand.

LILY: OK. So, thanks anyway. And I'm sorry I bothered you with all this stuff.

HALEY: Hey, no worries. Good luck though. Ya know — with Erick Von and everything.

LILY: Thanks. I'll try that visualization thingie — maybe it'll work.

HALEY: Hey Lily — could you maybe do *me* a favor?

LILY: Sure . . . I guess . . . I mean what could *I* possibly do for you?

HALEY: Well, now that you've talked with me and everything and you see I'm really no different than you or anyone else . . .

LILY: Yeah?

HALEY: Could you maybe just talk to some of the kids and tell them to stop calling me Harriet Potter every time I walk down the hall?

LILY: *(Laughing.)* Now *that* is something I can definitely fix! Without magic! Consider it done!

HALEY: What a relief! I'm sick of people trying to see if I have a scar on my forehead! *See!* No scar!

(They laugh together as HALEY shows LILY that she has no scar on her head.)

END OF SCENE

BLIND DATE

KIRSTEN has asked her boyfriend to set up a blind date for her best friend YASMIN. They all go out to dinner at a relatively nice restaurant. Unfortunately, the guy is a terrible slob so YASMIN and KIRSTEN escape to the restroom to figure out how to ditch him.

YASMIN: I'm not going back out there. I'm totally mortified.

KIRSTEN: You really think he's that bad?

YASMIN: Are you kidding me? He's a Neanderthal. He's disgusting!

KIRSTEN: Well, I did notice he sort of smells funny. I'm gonna kill Ricky. He told me his cousin was cute.

YASMIN: Ya know, I had a funny feeling. My instincts told me not to go on a blind date. But, of course, I was *trying* to be a good friend.

KIRSTEN: But I was trying to be a good friend to you. I thought it would be fun to go on a date together. And Ricky said he knew this great guy. He said he would fix up his own sister with this guy, but he can't 'cause . . . like . . . ya know . . . they're cousins!

YASMIN: Well, now we know how he really feels about his sister. *(Beat.)* What am I going to do? I can't go back out there. He *sucks* his fingers! If he does it again, I think I might barf right there at the table!

KIRSTEN: It was gross . . . but just to be fair . . . he was eating ribs. I mean, it's hard *not* to suck your fingers when you're eating ribs.

YASMIN: Hey! Whose side are you on?

KIRSTEN: Yours. I'm on yours. You're right . . . he's totally repulsive. There's gotta be a more polite way to eat ribs.

YASMIN: So how do I get out of this? We can't hide in the bathroom all night — although it *would* be more fun than going back out there.

KIRSTEN: We have to come up with a really believable lie because I don't want Ricky finding out you didn't really like his cousin.

YASMIN: Why not?

KIRSTEN: It'll hurt his feelings.

YASMIN: Oh give me a break! What about my feelings? Doesn't he know his cousin has the manners of a gorilla? And the personality of a wet towel? And the looks of a . . .

KIRSTEN: *(Interrupting.)* OK, OK . . . leave the poor guy alone.

YASMIN: I guess we *should* feel sorry for him, huh? He probably never goes out on dates. That's why he doesn't know how to act. Maybe he's never even eaten in a restaurant before. That would explain a lot.

KIRSTEN: I don't know. Ricky made it sound like he's one of the most popular kids at his school. He made it sound as if the guy has a new girlfriend every week and he'd been doing *us* a favor.

YASMIN: Well of course Ricky's gonna say that . . . he wanted to build him up. But it can't possibly be true, right? I mean, do you actually think there are girls out there who find him attractive?

KIRSTEN: Maybe if they like big hairy smelly guys who can barely speak in full sentences . . . if they like that, they'd like him.

YASMIN: How do I get out of this? I want to go home *now*. I'll just die if I have to look at this guy for one more minute, let alone have to sit with him in the backseat of the car. I feel like I'm never gonna get his stench out of my nose.

KIRSTEN: OK . . . here's my idea — do you have your phone with you?

YASMIN: Yeah.

KIRSTEN: Well call your mom and tell her to call you back in five minutes. Then act as if there's some huge emergency and you have to leave right away!

YASMIN: That's pretty good. But how do I get home?

KIRSTEN: We could all leave now and take you home.

YASMIN: Noooo! I'll have to sit with him in the car.

KIRSTEN: Ricky can take you. I'll stay here with Bigfoot.

YASMIN: Oh . . . I wouldn't want you to have to do that. You're a great friend, but that's too much to ask.

KIRSTEN: I don't mind.

YASMIN: Really? Are you sure? Doesn't he gross you out?

KIRSTEN: A little. But, I don't think he's that bad. My brother is worse. If I can stand lookin' at my brother, I can stand this.

YASMIN: Wow. You're amazing. Do you think Ricky will be mad?

KIRSTEN: Not if you're believable. Try to be as believable as possible. Can you cry?

YASMIN: Oh yeah. I can totally cry. I'll say my Aunt Lucy had to be rushed to the hospital and my mom needs me to be by her side.

KIRSTEN: Don't say that . . . what if your aunt Lucy really gets sick? That's bad luck.

YASMIN: No it's not . . . I don't even have an Aunt Lucy so it's OK. You better go back to the table before they get suspicious. I'll call my mom and then I'll be right out.

KIRSTEN: OK. Don't forget to start crying. And not too big — don't sob uncontrollably or anything . . . just a couple of tears rolling down your cheeks ought to convince them.

YASMIN: That'll be easy. All I have to do is look at my *beautiful* date; that's enough to make anyone cry!

END OF SCENE

FIVE-FINGER DISCOUNT

*BETH and JODI are friends shopping for makeup,
when BETH confesses to JODI that when she can't afford a particular item, she manages to obtain it her own
special way. She suggests that JODI try her method, but
JODI wants no part of it.*

JODI: Look at this color? It's great, isn't it? Or do you think
  it's too dark for me?

BETH: Try it on.

JODI: I can't try it on.

BETH: Well how are ya gonna know if it's the right color
  or not?

JODI: I always eyeball it.

BETH: Right, and how many crummy lipsticks do you have at
  home?

JODI: *(Laughing in agreement.)* Drawers full! I see your point,
  but ya can't just try it on. If I don't want it — how disgusting
  is that? I put it back and someone else picks it up and it
  has my lip germs all over it. Or worse — someone before
  me tried it on, put it back, and then *I* try it on and I get
  their lip germs — gross!!

BETH: So put it on the inside of your wrist — like this, see?
  (She demonstrates.)

JODI: Ohhhh — that's such a nice color. Hold your arm up to
  my face. What do you think?

BETH: It's definitely not too dark for you. It's great for your
  complexion. I think you should get it.

JODI: I can't get anything today — I'm totally broke.

BETH: So why should you let that stop you?

JODI: Well I hate to break it to you — but that's how stores
  work these days. They give you the thing you want to buy,
  and you give them this thing called money!

BETH: I'm saying just take it.

JODI: Shoplift?

BETH: You've never done it before?

JODI: *(Surprised.)* No! Never.

BETH: Come on!

JODI: No, I never have. I'd be too freaked out that I'd get caught. You've done it before?

BETH: Tons of times. It's totally easy. If you act cool, you can get away with anything.

JODI: I can't believe it.

BETH: Don't be such a prude.

JODI: I'm *not* a prude, Beth — I just don't see why you would need to shoplift.

BETH: It's a great rush. See these earrings? A little gift from that jewelry booth in the mall. And I hardly ever pay for nail polish or lipstick or any makeup for that matter. It's so easy to stick it in your pocket.

JODI: What will you do if you get caught?

BETH: I never will. I'm too good at it.

JODI: One day you're gonna get caught. Some camera will see you or some alarm will go off when you walk out of the store and you're gonna get busted. It's bound to happen. You should quit while you're ahead.

BETH: I told you — that will never happen. I'm too careful; I know how to work it. And besides, if I start getting bad vibes, I usually put it back before I walk out of the store. See, they can't bust you until you leave the store and if I feel like someone's suspicious and watching me — I don't take anything.

JODI: I think you're crazy. I couldn't do it. And it's just wrong, Beth. Stealing is wrong. Sorry if I sound like a priss, but I don't agree with you at all.

BETH: Well you want that lipstick, don't you?

JODI: Yes. But I can wait until I can afford to pay for it. And if I can't ever pay for it, then I don't need it that bad. I hope I never *need* anything bad enough that I'd have to steal it.

BETH: I don't need half the stuff I take, but I want it so I take it.

JODI: You can't just walk around taking things because you want them! I can't believe you. It's like you have no conscience or something.

BETH: What's that supposed to mean? You think I'm some social outcast now because I steal? Half our friends do it — just ask them. Where do you think Shelly got that new bracelet she's always showing off?

JODI: She said her grandmother gave it to her.

BETH: Yeah, right. I was with her when she took it. It was the same day I took these earrings. Wake up, Jodi — everyone steals.

JODI: It doesn't mean I have to. I can't believe you guys!

BETH: C'mon. Don't be mad. It's just some harmless fun. It's not like we're stealing cars or anything. We don't take anything big! Just whatever we can fit in our pocket.

JODI: I don't care if you steal a pack of gum — it's wrong. It will always be wrong. And I don't know how I can ever totally trust you guys again.

BETH: We would never steal from you!

JODI: How do I know that?

BETH: Because I'm your friend. And I just told you I never would — isn't that enough?

JODI: I don't know. Shelly lied about the bracelet. I never asked you where you got those earrings from, but if I had, would you have told me the truth?

BETH: I'm telling you now. And I think you're making too big a deal out of this.

JODI: Maybe you think it's no big deal — but I do. I'm sorry Beth, but I think it's wrong what you're doing. And I don't want any part of it. I'm gonna go.

BETH: Jodi! It's not worth losing a friendship over! Why are you being like this?

JODI: I'll see you later. I really don't want to talk to you right now.

BETH: *(Calling after her.)* You're overreacting!! *(She picks up the lipstick that JODI wanted and sticks it in her pocket.)* She can't stay mad at me, if I give her a little gift to make her feel better! *(She looks around to make sure no one saw her and exits.)*

END OF SCENE

DISAPPROVAL

SAMANTHA is upset because of her mother's disapproval of the boy she is dating. She has been told that she must stop seeing him, or drastic measures will be taken. Here, she explains to her friend KENDALL why her mother doesn't care for her boyfriend, Kyle.

KENDALL: I knew your mom was strict, but I never thought she'd go this far.

SAMANTHA: I have never seen her get so angry. It kind of freaked me out. But this whole situation is freaking me out. What do you think I should do?

KENDALL: Maybe she's bluffing. I can't believe she'd send you away from all your friends and family just because she doesn't like some guy you're dating.

SAMANTHA: I don't think she's bluffing. I think she'd really do it. She hates Kyle. Hates him with a capital H.

KENDALL: So talk to your dad. He wouldn't let her send you away.

SAMANTHA: Are you kidding? Dad's gonna do anything Mom tells him to do. Besides, he can't really believe that his little girl is dating boys. He still thinks I'm ten years old.

KENDALL: I know what you mean. My dad still treats me like a little girl too. He's in total denial, but I haven't really brought any guys home, so he still hasn't had to deal with it, ya know? *(Beat.)* Sam, why do you think your mom hates Kyle so much? He's one of the coolest guys I've ever known. I'd die to go out with him. He treats you OK, doesn't he?

SAMANTHA: You know why.

KENDALL: Seriously, I don't know. I was thinkin' maybe he was rude to her, but that doesn't sound like him. He's always so sweet. Then I was thinkin' maybe she caught you guys doing something you shouldn't have been doing . . . was that it?

SAMANTHA: It's not any of those things. It's because of his past.

KENDALL: What past?

SAMANTHA: He spent a couple of years in Juvi.

KENDALL: Are you kidding me?

SAMANTHA: Don't look so shocked . . . he's not some murderer or anything. He used to hang out with some lowlifes and he got caught with a bunch of drugs.

(KENDALL is surprised and doesn't know what to say.)

SAMANTHA: Don't look at me like that. You look like my mother. Why does everyone have to judge him? He made a mistake; he paid his debt to society and he's a great guy. I'm sick of having to defend him when he didn't do anything that bad.

KENDALL: I'm sorry . . . I'm sorry . . . I'm *not* being judgmental. I'm just surprised, that's all. I had no idea he used to be into all that. Makes him even more mysterious. But now I understand why your mom is flippin' out.

SAMANTHA: But ya know, she's such a hypocrite, because when she first met him she liked him a lot. She told me she thought we were a good match and she thought he was really charming — she was actually *happy* for me. And now, since she found out, she acts as if I'm dating some serial killer or something . . . she goes to me the other day . . . she goes *(In her mother's voice.)* "If that boy ever steps one foot into this house again, I'm shipping you off to another state."

KENDALL: That is so harsh. It's so not fair that she isn't giving Kyle a chance. He's such a great guy.

SAMANTHA: Tell me about it.

KENDALL: *(Hesitantly, she's curious, but she doesn't want to upset SAMANTHA.)* So . . . did he *take* drugs or just sell them?

SAMANTHA: Both, I think. But just for a little while. And he got busted at his old school — got caught selling dope in the bathroom and I think he was getting high with the kid he sold it to. So they sent him to Juvi for like two years and they put him through a rehab program and everything, and now he's totally clean. Got great grades last year . . . totally turned his life around. All the teachers love him; all the kids like him . . . everyone likes him, except my *mother!*

KENDALL: She's scared he's gonna turn you on to drugs.

SAMANTHA: If I wanted to do drugs, I wouldn't need Kyle to help me.

KENDALL: I know that, but she doesn't. She's scared, Sam. Can't you see that?

SAMANTHA: Don't take my mother's side, please!

KENDALL: I'm not. But I think you should lay low with Kyle for a while. Let your mom cool off. And maybe you could get *your* mom to talk to *his* mom and then she would know how hard he's been working to straighten his life out.

SAMANTHA: That *would* be a good idea, except that his mom doesn't exactly like me either. She thinks he should concentrate on school and not date at all. We're totally screwed.

KENDALL: But it's kind of romantic in a way. You guys are like Romeo and Juliet.

SAMANTHA: Yeah, and look how things turned out for them.

KENDALL: That's not even funny.

SAMANTHA: Look, I like Kyle and everything. I like him *a lot!* But I'm not the type to do something as stupid as kill myself over the guy or even run away with him. That's so lame. It's something that would happen in a TV movie.

KENDALL: So what *are* you going to do?

SAMANTHA: What can I do? Nothing! I don't really have any choice, do I? We'll see each other at school and that's gonna have to be enough for awhile. Maybe one of these days my mom will come to her senses. But there's no way I'm going to risk getting sent off to some out-of-state dorky boarding school. That's just *not* going to happen.

KENDALL: So . . . no more hanging out with Kyle after school? No more going to the movies? No more nothing?

SAMANTHA: Looks that way.

KENDALL: So, what if he gets tired of waiting for you and starts going out with somebody else?

SAMANTHA: Like who?

KENDALL: I don't know . . . but there's a lot of girls who like him. If they know he's available, they're gonna pounce. *(Pause as if she's thinking of this plan for the first time.)* Hey, I know! *I'll* go out with him and that way I'll be able to keep an eye on him until your mom agrees to let you date him again.

SAMANTHA: *(Reluctantly.)* I don't know. *(Beat.)* You really think other girls are gonna pounce?

KENDALL: *(Matter-of-factly.)* Yes . . . yes I do. I could be your safety net.

SAMANTHA: But won't your mom freak out if she finds out about his drug history?

KENDALL: Are you kidding? I think my mom will be thrilled that I'm finally going out with a guy! And if she does find out, I really don't think she'll care. She's not nearly as strict as your mom.

SAMANTHA: Well . . . I guess it could be a good idea. This way I won't have to totally give him up — I'll still be connected to him in some way. I'll be connected to him through you.

KENDALL: Yeah . . . I'll be your connection. I'll tell you everything you want to know. And I'll keep him very busy and away from all the other girls.

SAMANTHA: OK . . . well . . . I guess I should tell him about this plan; let him know that my mother's a freak and I can't be with him anymore.

KENDALL: No . . . you can't tell him. You can't risk getting caught. I'll tell him. I'll explain everything. Just leave this all to me. I'll take care of it. And I'm sure he'll understand too. I'm sure he wouldn't want you going off to Switzerland or wherever it is your mom would send you. At least he'll still get to see you every day at school.

SAMANTHA: Yeah . . . well, I guess this is the best solution.

Tell him I couldn't call him because my mom is monitoring my cell phone calls. And tell him that I miss him and tell him that . . .

KENDALL: *(Interrupting, anxious to get going.)* Yeah, yeah, I'll tell him everything. I'm gonna go find him now so don't worry about it. You can definitely count on me! See you later.

(KENDALL runs off. SAMANTHA looks after her uncertainly.)

 END OF SCENE

THE SECRET

KENSIE and CORINNE are sisters though they are nothing alike. CORINNE is a few years older; she is very pretty and popular. KENSIE is shy. She keeps to herself and does not have many friends, preferring to bury herself in books. The two girls don't care for each other too much. In this scene, CORINNE is thrilled to give her sister the news that KENSIE has always suspected and dreaded to hear.

CORINNE: *(Knocking on KENSIE'S door and opening it without waiting for an answer.)* Hey . . . you! I want to talk to you.

KENSIE: *(At her desk doing homework.)* Go away!

CORINNE: It's *very* important!

KENSIE: I don't care if you just got asked out on another date. Go away!

CORINNE: It's not about me. *(She takes a dramatic pause.)* It's about you.

KENSIE: *(Impatiently.)* What?

CORINNE: You're going to die when you hear.

KENSIE: Just tell me already, would you? Tell me and then get out. I've got a lot of work to do.

CORINNE: Well, I was looking around in Mom's closet trying to find some of those cool clothes she had when she was our age . . . she had this one purple sweater that was so cool, so seventies, ya know? And I wanted to wear it to the . . .

KENSIE: *(Interrupting angrily.)* What does this have to do with me, you idiot?!

CORINNE: You call me an idiot again and I'll black your eye.

KENSIE: Just *tell* me already.

CORINNE: Well, like I said, I was looking for the sweater. But what I found was this box. This very cool metal box and I thought if my mom wasn't using it, she'd let me have it.

KENSIE: *(Snickering.)* You said "my mom" like she's not my mom too.

CORINNE: Well . . . that's what I wanted to tell you.

KENSIE: *(Suspiciously.)* What?

CORINNE: Mom is not your mom. And Dad is not your dad. *(She takes another one of her dramatic pauses and then says triumphantly.)* You're adopted!

KENSIE: You're crazy. *(CORINNE continues to stand there smirking.)* Get out of here!

CORINNE: There were papers in that metal box, Kensie. I *read* them. They're adoption papers with your name and birthday on them. I always knew you weren't my real sister.

KENSIE: *(Shocked, she speaks more to herself than to CORINNE.)* I can't believe it. Why didn't they ever tell me?

CORINNE: They probably feel sorry for you.

KENSIE: Ya know what, Corinne? You can be such a little . . . such a little . . . oh, forget it.

CORINNE: *(Taunting.)* Such a little what? Come on, don't be such a wimp . . . say it!

KENSIE: Fine! You can be such a little *bitch*!

CORINNE: *(Laughing.)* Call me anything you want you little creep. It's not going to change the fact that we're not related. *(Dances around the room, planning her strategy.)* I'm so relieved. I can't wait to tell everyone at school!

KENSIE: You're going to tell your friends? Corinne, *please* don't do that.

CORINNE: Why not? I want everyone to know you and I are not really related as soon as possible.

KENSIE: I'm going to talk to Mom.

CORINNE: She's not your mom!

KENSIE: You're such a stupid idiot! They're *my* parents as much as they're yours. And I'm going to talk to them and find out exactly what is going on.

CORINNE: If you tell my mom I was snooping in her closet, I'll deny it. And even if you do tell her, who do you think she'll believe? Her *real* daughter, or her fake one?

KENSIE: You are *so* pathetic! Thank God we don't have the same genes!

CORINNE: What I don't understand is why they felt they needed to adopt you in the first place — I would have been perfectly happy being an only child. *(Starts to exit the room.)* You're not exactly the sister of my dreams.

(She exits. KENSIE sits stunned with the news.)

KENSIE: *(Calling after her.)* What do you think they're gonna do? Just ship me off some place because *you* don't want me as your sister? *(Thinking things over for a bit.)* Oh, God. Would they do that? Oh, God!

END OF SCENE

CLOSE CALL

After a party where some of the kids had been drinking, three students were killed in a car accident. ASHLEY is feeling incredibly guilty, because she had almost taken a ride in that fatal car. Here, she discusses the consequences with her friend NATASHA.

NATASHA: Do you realize that it could have been you that night?

ASHLEY: Of course I realize that. Why do you think I'm so freaked out?

NATASHA: What do you think your parents would do if they ever find out?

ASHLEY: I don't want to think about it. They almost didn't let me go to the party in the first place. I never begged so much in my life. And ever since the accident, they barely let me out of their sight.

NATASHA: I know. My mom's been extremely overprotective lately. I think everybody's parents are totally wiggin' out!

ASHLEY: If my mom ever found out that I was actually sitting in that car, she'd never let me out of this house again.

NATASHA: Ya gotta stop thinkin' about it. She never has to know cause you're safe now. Hey, what made you get out of there anyway?

ASHLEY: I forgot my purse. Can you believe it? I'm sitting in the backseat, so excited to be sitting next to Josh — and then I remembered my purse. I was going to just forget it, but I needed my house keys — so I told them to wait for me, I'd be right back, and by the time I came back, they had left.

NATASHA: And Christy had taken your place next to Josh. Wow.

ASHLEY: I was soooooo angry when I found out that she had gotten in the car. She knew how much I liked Josh and I couldn't believe she would do that to me. And now . . . God, I'm a horrible person. I feel like I wished this accident.

NATASHA: Don't do that to yourself. You didn't cause this. Tim had been drinking; he knew he shouldn't be driving. Josh had been drinking. For all you know, Christy was drinking. Everybody at that party is to blame. No one should have let them leave.

ASHLEY: Did you drink?

NATASHA: Nah. I can't stand how it tastes. I don't see what the appeal is. Did you?

ASHLEY: I'm an idiot.

NATASHA: Why? You did?

ASHLEY: I was trying to look cool for Josh. He offered me a sip of his beer, so I took it. I didn't really like the way it tasted either, but I liked the way he was looking at me. I'm so stupid.

NATASHA: You're not stupid.

ASHLEY: Yes I am. Sometimes I wish I *had* been in that car. Sometimes I wish it had been me that died instead of Christy.

NATASHA: *(Shocked.)* Are you nuts? Why would you say that? *(ASHLEY doesn't respond; NATASHA is truly concerned.)*

NATASHA: I think maybe you should see someone.

ASHLEY: Like a therapist or something?

NATASHA: Yeah. You're really beating yourself up over this. You gotta get a grip.

ASHLEY: *(Exploding.)* How can I get a grip? They're dead! All three of them are dead!! Doesn't that bother you? Doesn't that matter to you?

NATASHA: Yes, it definitely matters. But I'm not gonna blame myself. I'm not thinking it was my fault and I don't think you should either. It happened. It's awful. It's terrible. But we have to get on with our lives.

ASHLEY: It's easy for you to say . . . you weren't in love with any of them.

NATASHA: Neither were you.

ASHLEY: But I could have been. Josh might have been the love of my life and now we'll never know.

NATASHA: I guess not. I guess we'll never know. *(Pause — she doesn't know what else to say.)* Are you gonna be all right?

ASHLEY: I don't know. I guess so.

NATASHA: Do you want me to stay? I could probably get my mom to let me stay over.

ASHLEY: That's OK. I'm fine.

(NATASHA looks at her disbelievingly.)

ASHLEY: I promise. I'm fine. Maybe I will go talk to one of the counselors at school.

NATASHA: I really think you should. It was such a close call for you — I think it'll make you feel better.

ASHLEY: I don't think anything is going to make me feel better about this.

NATASHA: Well, at least it will help you deal with it.

ASHLEY: If I do, don't tell anyone, OK?

NATASHA: I wouldn't. But no one is going to think you're weird for talking to a shrink. You'd be surprised how many kids go. Especially now, after all this . . . *death.* Everyone's in crisis.

ASHLEY: I know, but still . . . don't tell anyone . . . I'd just rather you didn't.

NATASHA: *(She gestures as if she's buttoning her lips.)* My lips are sealed. *(Earnestly.)* I promise.

ASHLEY: Thanks. And thanks for coming over.

NATASHA: You're gonna be OK, ya know.

ASHLEY: I hope so. But I can't stop thinking about Josh, Tim, and Christy. It's never gonna be OK for them. I just can't believe they're gone.

NATASHA: Well, I know this sounds cheesy, but maybe it was their time. And you — getting out of that car when you did . . . it's not your time — you're not supposed to go yet. Cheesy, right?

ASHLEY: Yeah, but it helps. It makes sense. You're the best!

NATASHA: Hey, what are friends for?

(They hug.)

END OF SCENE

YEARBOOK PHOTOS

When TIFFANY has to have her wisdom teeth pulled on the same day as the yearbook photo is to be taken, her friend MEREDITH comes up with a plan to make sure TIFFANY'S photo will appear in the book.

MEREDITH: What are you wearing tomorrow?

TIFFANY: It doesn't matter . . . something grungy. I'll probably have blood and drool all over myself when it's over.

MEREDITH: What are you talking about? You have to wear something nice. At least on top!

TIFFANY: Why should I wear something nice to get my wisdom teeth pulled?

MEREDITH: No. For class pictures. We're taking yearbook pics tomorrow. Didn't you remember?

TIFFANY: Oh no! I can't. I'm getting my wisdom teeth out tomorrow.

MEREDITH: Well you'll have to postpone it.

TIFFANY: I can't! They're killing me — they've been killing me and I already had to wait a month to get this appointment.

MEREDITH: This is bad, Tif. Your cheeks are gonna be swollen for like a week!

TIFFANY: I know.

MEREDITH: You're gonna look like a chipmunk.

TIFFANY: I know!

MEREDITH: There's gonna be an empty slot in the yearbook above your name that says "no photo available."

TIFFANY: You're really making me feel great about all this — what a pal!

MEREDITH: Well it's serious! If you miss taking your yearbook photo, you're gonna regret it for the rest of your life. Your kids will think you were a loser. Your grandkids will say, "Where's Nana?" Didn't she go to high school?

TIFFANY: All right! You made your point! But if I don't get these

teeth out, my head is gonna explode. They're impacted —
coming in on top of my other teeth and the pain is unbelievable. Why do you think babies cry all the time? It's amazing that we ever survive teething.

MEREDITH: So you're not gonna get the picture taken? Tif —
there's gotta be a way to do both.

TIFFANY: I can't. The appointment is early. By the time I'm
supposed to get my picture taken I'll be so swelled up it'll
look like I swallowed a couple of grapefruits. I don't care.
I just won't ever show my kids my yearbook.

MEREDITH: I've got an idea.

TIFFANY: What? Have the photographer come to the dentist's
office?

MEREDITH: Don't be silly. You have the pictures from my
birthday party, right?

TIFFANY: Yeah, of course.

MEREDITH: There was a great one of you; a close-up shot and
you looked beautiful.

TIFFANY: Oh thanks.

MEREDITH: I'll go to your photo appointment and hold up
that picture. I'll cover my face with your photo and it will
be just as if you were there and that way you'll have this
great, awesome picture in this year's yearbook.

TIFFANY: That's the dumbest thing I've ever heard.

MEREDITH: Well it's better than having a blank space above
your name. Or having your picture taken with chipmunk
cheeks. It's a good idea, Tif. You look great in that picture.

TIFFANY: Do you think they'll let you do it?

MEREDITH: Will they let me do it? Look who you're talking
to! I can talk anyone into anything. Besides, I know all those
guys on the yearbook staff — they'll let me do it.

TIFFANY: I guess it is better than no picture at all.

MEREDITH: Yeah, it'll be great . . . it's totally a good idea. It
will definitely work.

TIFFANY: OK. Let's do it. I'll get you the picture.

MEREDITH: Awesome! And tomorrow afternoon, after the photo appointment, I'm gonna bring you some ice cream!

TIFFANY: I'm not getting my tonsils out!

MEREDITH: I know. But you'll only be able to eat soft food. I'll bring you a milkshake — that's all my sister could have when she had her wisdom teeth out. She gained like five pounds.

TIFFANY: Great. Just what I need.

MEREDITH: Should I bring you one?

TIFFANY: I don't care. Just whatever you do, *don't* bring a camera!

END OF SCENE

OLD FRIENDS

ANDREA and JACKIE were once best friends, but cir-
cumstances led to the end of their friendship. After sev-
eral months of not speaking, they run into each other
at the mall and finally thrash out their differences.

ANDREA: Hey Jackie, long time no see! How are you?
   (JACKIE looks pointedly at ANDREA but continues
   walking.)
ANDREA: Uh . . . *hello!* Jackie! *(Still no response.)* I didn't re-
   member that you were so *rude!*
   (JACKIE turns abruptly around and finally answers
   ANDREA.)
JACKIE: Rude? You think *I'm* rude!! That's the funniest thing
   I've heard all day.
ANDREA: What are you talking about?
JACKIE: Awww . . . she *forgot!!* How convenient!
ANDREA: Look, I haven't the faintest idea what you're talk-
   ing about — and I don't get why you're acting all mad and
   everything.
JACKIE: Well, let me refresh your sorry little memory. Two
   months ago — a girl named Gabby moved in next door to
   you. Instant pals, buddies, best friends. Out with the old
   and in with the new! You dumped me so fast, I thought I
   had been hit by a truck. It was *you* that was rude, Andrea.
   I'll never forget how you treated me and now you're acting as if nothing happened. You're unbelievable.
ANDREA: Oh that. Yeah, well — I didn't drop you! You said
   you didn't like Gabby. You stopped hanging around with us.
JACKIE: That's the whole point! We've been friends forever and
   in no time, this girl moves in and suddenly it's "Gabby this"
   and "Gabby that." "Oh, Gabby already saw that movie,"
   or "Gabby says shopping is boring." Or "I can't spend the
   night at your house, Jackie, 'cause I'm helping Gabby fix

up her room." I felt like a piece of garbage. You treated me like trash. Total trash. And I think the thing that hurts the most is that you don't even realize you did it.

ANDREA: Why didn't you ever tell me?

(JACKIE gives her a dirty look.)

ANDREA: OK, OK, I guess on some level I knew I wasn't treating you so great. But I really liked Gabby and she felt like the new girl. I didn't want her to be left out of stuff.

JACKIE: So you sacrificed me! You left *me* out of stuff! You totally killed our friendship.

ANDREA: Oh be fair, Jackie. It wasn't just me. You started backing away from me even before Gabby moved in.

JACKIE: That is so not true.

ANDREA: Well, that's how I remember it. You wanted to hang out with Freddy more. I was very understanding — new boyfriend and all. But in a way, I felt like I was losing you to him. So when Gabby moved in, it seemed like the perfect solution.

JACKIE: You have a very interesting memory. I never chose Freddy over you. I always included you whether I was with Freddy or not.

ANDREA: Yeah — that's real fun. Going out with your best friend *and* her boyfriend. Ever hear of the expression "Three's a crowd"?

JACKIE: But it wasn't like that. It was like three friends together, not you and a couple.

ANDREA: That's your opinion.

JACKIE: Oh, you're saying that you didn't have fun when the three of us did stuff together?

ANDREA: I always felt like a third wheel.

JACKIE: So why didn't you ever say anything to me about it?

ANDREA: *(She shrugs.)* I don't know. You were having so much fun with him — I didn't want to ruin it.

JACKIE: You wouldn't have ruined it. We would have figured something out. *(Pause.)* I'm sorry you felt like a third wheel.

ANDREA: Well, I'm sorry I treated you like crap when Gabby moved in.

JACKIE: So, where is Gabby? I thought she hated shopping.

ANDREA: Who knows where she is? We don't really hang out too much anymore. Once she started meeting other people, she pretty much blew me off. Karma, right?

JACKIE: I guess. I never trusted that girl; I can't say I'm surprised.

ANDREA: Oh, well . . . she was starting to bug me anyway! So, where's Freddy?

JACKIE: Playing basketball with the guys.

ANDREA: How's it going for you two?

JACKIE: Good! Really good. I think he's amazing. *(Self-consciously.)* I guess it could be love — I don't know. He's great.

ANDREA: Well I'm really happy for you, Jacks.

JACKIE: *(Smiling.)* No one else ever calls me that.

ANDREA: Well, we do have history, that's for sure.

JACKIE: So what are you doing now?

ANDREA: Just hanging out at the mall . . . spending money I don't have!

JACKIE: Ya wanna go get something to eat?

ANDREA: Now?

JACKIE: Yeah. Or we can go catch a movie if ya want to. I've got no other plans. We could just hang out, if you want to.

ANDREA: Just like old times, huh? No Gabby.

JACKIE: No Freddy.

ANDREA: I'd like that. I've missed ya, Jacks.

JACKIE: Yeah . . . I've missed you too!

(They hug and walk off together chatting like the two old friends that they are.)

END OF SCENE

GAME PLAN

SYDNEY tries to convince her best friend JESSICA that her plans for crashing a party will help her win the affections of a boy she has a crush on.

SYDNEY: You have to help me — this is the most important thing that has ever happened to me — so everything has to be perfect.

JESSICA: I'll try Syd, but I'm not sure how I can help. What exactly do you want me to do?

SYDNEY: Make me over. Make me look beautiful. Make me look like . . . make me look like you!

JESSICA: Shut up!

SYDNEY: I'm not kidding. I would die to have your looks. Just do whatever it takes to try and make me look as great as possible.

JESSICA: You already look good, Syd.

SYDNEY: Oh please . . . you don't have to kiss my butt . . . I know how I look.

JESSICA: I'm not kissing your butt! I happen to think you're very cute.

SYDNEY: *(Sarcastically.)* Cute! Great. Just what I want to be for the rest of my life! Cute.

JESSICA: What's wrong with cute?

SYDNEY: Cute is fine when you're a little kid. It doesn't cut it when you're trying to impress a guy. Especially a guy like Neal.

JESSICA: But he obviously likes you — I mean, he asked you on a date, didn't he?

SYDNEY: *(Reluctantly.)* Well, it isn't exactly a date . . . exactly.

JESSICA: But he asked you out, right?

SYDNEY: Well . . . not really.

JESSICA: Sydney! Do you or don't you have a date with Neal Carter tonight?

SYDNEY: Not an official date.

JESSICA: Well what is going on? You said this was the most important night of your life. So if you don't have an official date, what do you have?

SYDNEY: There's a party at Leigh Howard's house and he said he was going and he asked me if I would be there.

JESSICA: Leigh Howard invited you to her party?

SYDNEY: No. Not exactly. But what would be the harm if I just showed up? There'll be so many kids there, she won't even notice.

JESSICA: Did you tell Neal you weren't invited?

SYDNEY: I told him that I might show up.

JESSICA: Syd, you can't just go crashing some party.

SYDNEY: Why not? He *asked* me if I'd be there, which means he *wants* me to be there, which means I *have* to be there! This is a major opportunity, Jess, don't you see that?

JESSICA: I just don't think you should go chasing after some guy by going to a party that you weren't even invited to.

SYDNEY: That's easy for you to say, guys ask you out all the time. But this is the first time any guy has ever showed the slightest bit of interest in me and I think I would be pretty stupid if I didn't do something about it. I thought if anyone would be supportive, it would be you.

JESSICA: I want to be supportive, Syd, but I also don't want you making a fool out of yourself either.

SYDNEY: How would I be making a fool out of myself? How?

JESSICA: By showing up to Leigh's party. If she wanted you to come, she would have asked you. But she didn't. That should tell you something.

SYDNEY: What? What should it tell me?

JESSICA: Think about it.

SYDNEY: Well, I'm not surprised that I wasn't invited. We're not exactly *friends*. But we talk sometimes. Every now and then. It wouldn't have killed her to ask me. I know a lot of kids are going. Susie, Lindsey . . . they told me they'd be there. Did she ask you?

JESSICA: No way . . . I can't stand Leigh Howard and she knows it. She's such a little phony. I wouldn't go to her party even if she *had* invited me. And I don't think you should go either!

SYDNEY: But I have to go. Neal wants me there.

JESSICA: God, sometimes you're sooooo dense. Neal may want *you* there, but Leigh wants Neal there.

SYDNEY: How do you know?

JESSICA: Why do you think she asked him? Haven't you ever noticed how much she throws herself at him? She's constantly making a jerk out of herself whenever he's around. She's dying to go out with him . . . I actually think she's throwing this party just as an excuse to get him over to her house. She wouldn't even care if anyone else showed up. She must know you like him, that's why she didn't invite you.

SYDNEY: How could she know I like him; you're the only one I told. Did you say anything? I'll kill you if you said anything.

JESSICA: Of course I didn't say anything. But, Syd . . . it's kind of obvious — the way you act around him and stuff.

SYDNEY: Really?

JESSICA: Yeah.

SYDNEY: *(Bashfully.)* I can't help it. He's . . . I don't know . . . he's amazing.

JESSICA: Well . . . Leigh must have picked up on it and she's threatened by you — she doesn't want the competition.

SYDNEY: *(Excitedly.)* I can't believe it! I'm the competition! That is so cool. Now I definitely have to go.

JESSICA: But she's gonna kill you if she sees you there. Are you sure you know what you're doing? This could get really ugly, ya know.

SYDNEY: I don't care. I will fight for my man! *(Giggling.)* This is so exciting — nothing like this has ever happened to me before.

JESSICA: I think you're crazy.

SYDNEY: I'm just trying to live a little that's all. Nothing good will ever happen if I just sit at home and watch TV and day-dream about Neal liking me. Now will you help me get ready or not?

JESSICA: I'll help you, I'll help you . . . I just hope this all works out OK.

SYDNEY: *(Giggling again.)* Yeah, me too! But whatever happens, watch out, Leigh Howard, cause this is *my* night. God, I'm so excited! This is definitely gonna be an adventure!

JESSICA: *(Sarcastically.)* Oh . . . definitely!

END OF SCENE

Scenes for
Two Males

GOLDEN

*TREVOR and TYLER are best friends; however, TRE-
VOR has a reputation for sometimes overstepping his
bounds and taking advantage of TYLER'S friendship
and generosity. Here, once again TREVOR is asking his
buddy for a loan, but TYLER has become wise to his
fast-talking ways, and knowing he will never get the
money back, he refuses to lend a helping hand.*

TREVOR: Hey look . . . I can *get* the tickets. There isn't any
problem getting the tickets . . . the problem is *paying* for
the tickets.

TYLER: I told you forget it. I don't have that kind of money.
And I'm not that crazy about that band anyway.

TREVOR: Well . . . you don't have to go. Just lend me the cash
so I can go.

TYLER: Oh, that's very funny.

TREVOR: What's so funny about it?

TYLER: *Me* lending *you* money!

TREVOR: I'm good for it, man.

TYLER: Right. You're good for it. *(Getting out a small black
book and thumbing through it.)* Hmmm . . . let's see . . .
that's what you said when I lent you ten bucks last week.
Twenty-five bucks last month. Oh yeah . . . you were also
good for *another* twenty-five dollars back in November. And
I almost forgot about that five I slipped you yesterday when
we were at Starbucks.

TREVOR: You keep records?! You write it all down? Man, that
is truly anal. You need to get out more.

TYLER: *(Ignoring the comment.)* If you ever wind up paying
me back all the money you *say* you're good for, I'll probably be able to pay for my entire college education.

TREVOR: What if I promise that this will be the very last time
I ask you?

TYLER: That's what you always say.

TREVOR: I really need to go to this concert.

TYLER: How can you *need* to go to a concert? You *need* food; you *need* sleep. You don't *need* a concert.

TREVOR: I kinda promised Julie I would take her.

TYLER: I kind of figured it had somethin' to do with a girl.

TREVOR: Then you see how important this is.

TYLER: Whatever happened to Caroline?

TREVOR: Who?

TYLER: Caroline? The girl you *had* to take to dinner. *(TREVOR looks puzzled.)*

TYLER: The twenty-five dollars you borrowed last month?

TREVOR: Ohhhh . . . yeah. Caroline! Uh . . . ya know, that didn't work out too well.

TYLER: What did you do? Make her leave the tip?

TREVOR: Yeah, funny. Look this girl is different. Julie . . . she's *wow*, ya know. I mean she's . . . *whoa!* When I told her I had tickets to the concert she was all *over* me!

TYLER: But you don't have tickets!

TREVOR: Hey, we're just going round in circles here. *(As if he were explaining something difficult to a very small child.)* That's why I need the money, bro!

TYLER: You are unbelievable! I am not your personal ATM machine.

TREVOR: What do I have to do to get the money from you today?

TYLER: You're seriously starting to sound like a used car salesman. It's very scary.

TREVOR: C'mon . . . what will it take?

TYLER: It'll take a frickin' miracle, that's what!

TREVOR: How about I set you up with Julie's sister?

TYLER: What is she . . . twelve?

TREVOR: Hey man, I wouldn't do that to you!

TYLER: Forget it Trev. I'm busted. Flat broke. *(Showing empty wallet.)* Nada!

TREVOR: So what am I gonna do?

TYLER: Try telling her the truth. I know that's a new concept for you, but maybe you should try it.

TREVOR: *(Thinking it over.)* Hey . . . ya know . . . maybe that's not a bad idea. I tell her the truth . . . she feels bad for me . . . for us . . . that we're not going . . . she offers to pay for the tickets and I'm golden!

TYLER: *(Sarcastically.)* Slightly tarnished maybe, but golden.

TREVOR: *(Slapping him on the back.)* Thanks man. Great idea. Telling the truth. This will totally work — I am there! *(Starts to leave.)* Catch you later . . . and hey, I'll find out if Julie even has a sister. *(TREVOR exits.)*

TYLER: *(Shaking his head in amazement.)* Unbelievable! The guy is absolutely unbelievable!

END OF SCENE

THE BUSINESS PROPOSITION

KEVIN and SCOTT are two friends living in an average middle-class suburb. When SCOTT becomes increasingly generous as far as offering to lend him money, KEVIN discovers the truth about the way SCOTT earns his fortune.

KEVIN: I found the coolest camera in this thrift shop downtown. It's amazing. It's old school. No auto-focus crap here . . . the real deal.

SCOTT: Did you get it?

KEVIN: They want three hundred bucks for it, man. I mean it's totally worth it. It's kind of a rare camera that they don't make anymore. And the guy was even gonna offer to throw in a few lenses. It's a great deal. What am I talking about, it's an amazing deal! But . . . not for me.

SCOTT: Sounds like you can't afford to pass it up.

KEVIN: That's the problem . . . I can't *afford* it at all.

SCOTT: Dude, how do you expect to ever become a great photographer if you don't have the right equipment?

KEVIN: I don't have the money, man.

SCOTT: Ask your parents.

KEVIN: Fat chance. My dad would die if he knew I was interested in photography. He thinks anything artistic is a waste of time. To him, the only worthwhile professions are doctors and accountants.

SCOTT: Well, how much *do* you have?

KEVIN: Nothing. Fifty bucks tops.

SCOTT: So all you need is two fifty? You can come up with two fifty. That's nothing!

KEVIN: *(Sarcastically.)* Oh, yeah. Two fifty is nothing. What am I supposed to do? Snap my fingers and it'll magically appear? It might as well be two thousand and fifty. I can't get my hands on that kind of money. By the time I get it, that camera will be long gone.

SCOTT: *(Casually.)* I can get it for ya. A *loan* of course. I'd need it back. But if you want it that bad, we can go get that camera for you *today!*

KEVIN: You've got three hundred dollars?

SCOTT: Yep.

KEVIN: You've got three hundred dollars that you could lend me *right now?*

SCOTT: It's under my mattress as we speak.

KEVIN: Cash?

SCOTT: Dude! How many ways do I have to say it? I've got the dough; do you want it or not?

KEVIN: How do you have that kind of money?

SCOTT: C'mon, man. You know how I make my cash.

KEVIN: Well it ain't from mowing lawns, that's for sure.

SCOTT: You don't know?

KEVIN: No Scott, I have no clue. *(Mockingly.)* What are you, some big-time drug dealer?

SCOTT: Well I'm not exactly big-time, but I'm doing OK.

KEVIN: Are you *kidding* me?

SCOTT: Hey dude, don't I always have the *best?*

KEVIN: But I didn't know you sold. I didn't know you have your own little business. God, it's just like that movie.

SCOTT: Don't be so shocked, Kev. Gotta have somebody working the 'burbs. Why not me?

KEVIN: Because it's dangerous. You could get busted.

SCOTT: Oh please. It's about as dangerous as crossing the street in rush-hour traffic. And getting caught? Well, ya take your chances. It's worth it. It's totally worth it. You'll never see *me* flipping burgers at the In 'n Out.

KEVIN: But I don't know when I'll be able to pay you back. *I'm* gonna have to get a job at In 'n Out.

SCOTT: It's cool. Make payments. Gimme what you can on a weekly basis till you pay it off. I know how much you want that camera, man. You should be able to get it.

KEVIN: God, it's tempting. It's so tempting.

SCOTT: So . . . what's stopping you?

KEVIN: You're such a businessman. It kills me — making deals — negotiating payments. Your parents must be very proud.

SCOTT: Oh yeah, they're beaming with pride over my entrepreneurial skills. So what's it gonna be, man? Do you want the loan or not? Interest free . . . we can go get that camera right now. You're never gonna get a better offer than this.

KEVIN: Well . . . it's just that . . . look, just tell me straight out — if I don't pay you back right away, are you gonna have me whacked?

SCOTT: *(Laughing.)* Oh buddy, you really *do* watch too much television.

KEVIN: You didn't answer my question.

SCOTT: Dude, I sell a little weed. It's not that big a deal.

KEVIN: So you won't make me wear cement shoes and throw me in the river?

SCOTT: What did you do, watch *The Godfather* last night?

KEVIN: OK, OK, I'm overreacting. *(Pause.)* All right. Go get the money. I'll take you up on the offer.

SCOTT: Cool. Now you're thinking.

KEVIN: And I'll pay you back as soon as possible.

SCOTT: Yeah, you will.

KEVIN: And no funny business if I miss a payment, right?

SCOTT: *(Like a stereotypical tough guy.)* Yeah . . . I'll send my goons after you. Geez, lighten up will ya? You have definitely gotta get out more.

END OF SCENE

RITE OF PASSAGE

*TONY is encouraging his friend LOUIS to go buy him-
self a box of condoms. LOUIS is feeling embarrassed,
but TONY is convinced that buying condoms is an
experience every guy needs to go through — a rite of
passage.*

TONY: What's the big deal? Just go in there like you do this
everyday. That guy at the counter isn't gonna say anything
to you. He doesn't care.

LOUIS: If it's not such a big deal, then why can't you do this
for me?

TONY: Because you gotta do it yourself, dude. You gotta pay
your dues. No one bought me my first pack of condoms.

LOUIS: *(Looking around a little paranoid.)* Shut up! You don't
have to announce it to the world, ya know.

TONY: I don't know what you're stressing out about. It's not
illegal. It's not like you're trying to buy cigarettes or beer.
You're actually doing a good thing, ya know. You're taking charge . . . being responsible.

LOUIS: Responsible? Responsible for what? I don't even have
a girlfriend.

TONY: All the more reason that you should do this now. There's
no pressure — if you don't get the right kind — so what?
No harm, no foul. When the right time comes, you'll be
ready!

LOUIS: I don't know. I don't know why I have to do this now.

TONY: It's a practice run, man. Can't you see that?

LOUIS: Not exactly.

TONY: OK — let me paint you this picture. In a couple of
months, you find yourself dating some great chick. Things
start to progress. Then one night, you're sure you're gonna
score — she wants it, you definitely want it, and what happens — you have to stop because you're not prepared!

Because you were too scared to go into the drugstore and buy a harmless little box of rubbers.

LOUIS: I see your point.

TONY: Do you?

LOUIS: Yeah. I really do. But I can't exactly see something like that happening to me.

TONY: Oh come on, man. Of course it's gonna happen. It's just a matter of time.

LOUIS: Is that . . . like . . . how it happened for you?

TONY: How what happened?

LOUIS: Ya know. You bought them way ahead of time and when the moment of truth arrived, you were ready, willing and able?

TONY: Well . . . uh . . . yeah . . . sure . . . I guess.

LOUIS: You guess? It either did or it didn't.

TONY: Well I'm positive that that's how it's *gonna* go down when the time comes.

LOUIS: When the time comes?! You mean you haven't . . . you didn't . . . you're still . . . Awwww, man!

TONY: Hey dude, I'm waitin' for the right girl. I don't take this sort of thing lightly, ya know.

LOUIS: What a freakin' liar! You're such a phony. Making it seem like you're this major stud with all this experience.

TONY: *(Calmly.)* Hey now . . . I *never* said I had all this experience. Not in that department anyway. I said I had experience buying condoms. Buying condoms is a breeze. I've got quite a stockpile now. I could go to a desert island for an entire week with the most gorgeous woman on the planet and I'd be totally prepared. Various sizes and colors too. I'm stylin'!

LOUIS: Then just give me one of your boxes.

TONY: No! No way. This is a rite of passage. Ya gotta do it yourself. Now go — start working on building your own collection. I can only think that you're gonna thank me for this one day.

LOUIS: I can't believe you've never even put one to the test. I'm not sure I should be taking anymore of your advice.

TONY: Suit yourself. But don't come knocking on my door at two in the morning because you're desperate for protection. I'm not gonna be some twenty-four hour convenience store for you. I'm telling you, the smart thing is to start stocking up NOW! You could meet the girl of your dreams tonight, and then where will you be?

LOUIS: You have a very active fantasy life, don't you.

TONY: That's what separates us from the animals, dude. So are you doing this or not?

LOUIS: OK, OK. You do have a point. Once I get it over with the first time, it'll always be easy after that.

TONY: Exactly.

LOUIS: You coming in with me?

TONY: I told you, man, you're on your own.

LOUIS: All right. I'll do this thing. I guess it won't be too terrible. Wait here for me then, OK.

TONY: Rock on! And hey . . . congratulations, bro! Today you are a man!

LOUIS: Yeah . . . right. You're nuts! I'll be a man the day I actually use one of 'em. If that day ever comes!

TONY: Sooner than you think, my man! Sooner than you think! (LOUIS enters the store. TONY leans against the wall feeling quite pleased with himself.)

END OF SCENE

THE TEST

GREG *has secretly gotten an advanced copy of his history midterm and is now trying to persuade his buddy MICHAEL that using it to pass the test is their only hope of getting a passing grade in the class.*

GREG: You're not gonna believe what I got my hands on.

MICHAEL: Tickets to the play-offs?

GREG: Very funny . . . you wish! No man, something even better.

MICHAEL: What's better than basketball play-offs?

GREG: *(Pulling some paper out of his backpack.)* Check it out.

MICHAEL: What is it?

GREG: What is it? *What is it?* It's only the history midterm. How cool is that?

MICHAEL: Wait a minute. You're telling me you are now holding in your hands the midterm exam for history class? The one we're supposed to be studying for right now? The one I'm gonna fail tomorrow morning?

GREG: The one and only.

MICHAEL: Score!

GREG: No kidding!

MICHAEL: How'd you manage to get that?

GREG: As you know my girl works in the administration office. Mr. Shaw comes in with a stack of tests and lays them on the counter. Then he goes off to check his mailbox and then Annie said his cell phone rang and he got very involved in some conversation. Meanwhile, no one else was around . . . so she lifted one off the top of the stack. I swear, I'm gonna have to marry that girl!

MICHAEL: That was incredibly bold.

GREG: She's very, very cool.

MICHAEL: So . . . did she get the answer sheet too?

GREG: That would be too much to ask for. But we have the

questions, Mike! We'll look up the answers in the book; it won't take too much time at all. We'll totally ace that test tomorrow. Life is good!

MICHAEL: Well, congratulations man! I'm really happy for ya. But I gotta go.

GREG: What are you talking about? Where you going? We have a test to prepare for.

MICHAEL: I know; that's what I'm going to do.

GREG: *(Waving the test in front of him.)* Well let's work on this together — c'mon, we'll go to my house.

MICHAEL: Nope.

GREG: Huh?

MICHAEL: I'm not gonna cheat on this test, Greg.

GREG: Why not?

MICHAEL: I just can't. It's wrong. And besides, what if that's not the right test. How do you know that's the midterm for our class?

GREG: It says so right here on the top. *(Reading.)* "World History Midterm Exam, Periods 1, 2, 5, 6." It's the real deal, man. You're really lame if you don't take advantage of this amazing opportunity.

MICHAEL: I know. But it doesn't feel right somehow. It feels too easy.

GREG: That's the point. We want it to be easy.

(MICHAEL is quiet; he obviously is conflicted and doesn't know what to do.)

GREG: Let me ask you something.

MICHAEL: What?

GREG: Are you gonna study all night for this test?

MICHAEL: Not *all* night. But I'll study a little. But there's no way I can learn six weeks of work in one night.

GREG: So are you gonna pass it?

MICHAEL: Probably not. I haven't taken very good notes and I haven't read any of the chapters. I'll cram as much as I can. And I'll eat a Snickers bar before the test tomorrow — I read somewhere that chocolate is good for your memory.

GREG: Why are you making it so hard on yourself?

MICHAEL: Because I'll get caught if I cheat.

GREG: How? How will anyone ever know? There's no possible way we can get caught. No one knows we have this test!

MICHAEL: Except for Annie.

GREG: She's not gonna say anything. She's my girl!

MICHAEL: Shaw's gonna think it's awfully strange that two slackers like us ace this test. He hates me anyway — there'll be an investigation, I just know it.

GREG: So . . . we won't ace it. We won't answer every question right. We'll still get a decent grade on the thing and he won't be suspicious.

MICHAEL: He'll be suspicious unless I fail it.

GREG: Mike, man, c'mon . . . even if he does get suspicious, he won't be able to prove a thing. He'll think you actually studied. And ya know, in a way, we're gonna study — 'cause we have to look up the answers anyway, we might actually learn something.

MICHAEL: That's a good point.

GREG: So, you're in?

MICHAEL: *(Reluctantly.)* I don't think so, man. I just can't take the chance. If I cheat on this test, ya know what that will mean, don't you?

GREG: What?

MICHAEL: *(Working himself up into a frenzy.)* We'd have to get Annie to steal the final for us too! And pop quizzes! What about all those pop quizzes Shaw likes to give? It's too complicated and I just know I'd get caught.

GREG: Mike, calm down! You're out of control. Having a copy of this test was supposed to chill you out, not flip you out. Just do yourself a favor . . . worry about one test at a time. And right now, you don't have to worry about this midterm. It's up to you.

MICHAEL: I can't do it. I can't go through with it. It's too much pressure. Look Greg, you're secret is safe with me. I won't tell a soul. But I'm not up for cheatin'. It's just too risky.

GREG: You're sure?

MICHAEL: Oh yeah. I've already got an ulcer thinking about it. Some people are just not made for cheating. I guess I'm one of them. Good luck to you though. I'll see ya tomorrow. But now I better go hit the books.

END OF SCENE

COMPANY MAN

ZACK has become shift manager at a fast-food restaurant. DEREK thinks because they're friends, it will be a sure way for him to get a job. But ZACK takes his position very seriously and is not willing to simply give the job away to anyone.

DEREK: This is so cool. *You* interviewing *me*. It sure is good to have friends in high places.

ZACK: *(Business-like.)* Yeah. I guess . . . So, where's your application?

DEREK: Are you kidding? You want me to fill out that dumb-ass application?

ZACK: Yeah, I do. I gotta have the paperwork. If you're hired, we'll need it to process you.

DEREK: *If* I'm hired? Oh, I get it. We have to play it all legit. Let the higher-ups see that you're doing this manager thing right.

ZACK: Well, yeah . . . there's that. But to interview you for the job, I need a completed job application. See your experience and stuff like that.

DEREK: Dude! It's me! You already know everything you need to know. I'm waiting for you to tell me when to start!

ZACK: You haven't gotten the job yet.

DEREK: Hey, I thought this was a done deal.

ZACK: Derek, I told you there was an opening here on my shift. I told you to come in and apply for the job. *Apply.* I never said you had the job. There's like six people applying for this job. I can't just give it to you because I know you.

DEREK: Well that's usually what friends do for each other. Help each other. Man, you *know* I need this gig.

ZACK: Then fill out the application and get interviewed like everyone else. The best person gets the job.

DEREK: I can't believe you're being such a hard-ass. This manager thing has really gone to your head.

ZACK: I'm just trying to do my job. They promoted me because I don't slack off. I'm responsible and I take all this very seriously.

DEREK: A little too seriously, if you ask me. It's a fast-food place for crying out loud — not some bank on Wall Street.

ZACK: If it's *only* a fast-food place, then why do you want to work here so bad?

DEREK: 'Cause I thought I could cut through all the crap because I had a connection. I *thought* my buddy would help me out in a time of need.

ZACK: Well, I'm not gonna just hand this job to you, Derek. I worked really hard to make shift manager. I'm not gonna blow it by hiring someone who thinks he can screw around all day because he happens to "have a connection." Don't take advantage of me like that, man.

DEREK: Oh, I have to swear to uphold the company oath, is that it? Thou shalt not sneak French fries at break time?

ZACK: Sorry, Derek, but it seems pretty obvious that you're definitely not cut out to work here.

DEREK: *(Unbelievingly.)* You're like a frickin' robot! What did this place do to you, man?

ZACK: Made me appreciate a hard-earned dollar.

DEREK: Who are you, my *Dad*?!

ZACK: *(Standing and walking toward the door.)* Thanks for stopping by, Derek. I wish you the best of luck.

DEREK: So that's it? You're dismissing me? You're not gonna let me work in this crappy place because you have too much *integrity?!*

ZACK: It doesn't seem to be suited to you. I think you'd be happier working someplace else.

DEREK: This is unreal. You're scary, man. As soon as you put on that uniform you turn into someone I really don't want to know. You even talk different.

ZACK: I've got some other people to interview, so . . .

DEREK: *(Looking around.)* Are there cameras? Is this a "Twilight Zone" episode?

ZACK: If you fill out an application, I'll review it and get back to you in a couple of days.

DEREK: Screw it — I don't need this job that much! I'd like to stay *human* if ya don't mind!

(He exits loudly as ZACK shrugs and returns to the desk.)

END OF SCENE

ROLE MODEL

When he realizes his older brother JORDAN is still in bed sleeping, MAX questions him as to why he's not going to school that day and insists he become someone more responsible so that MAX has someone to look up to.

MAX: How come you're still in bed?

JORDAN: How come you're buggin' me?

MAX: How come?

JORDAN: I'm *trying* to sleep and if you'd stop talking to me that would really help a lot.

MAX: Don't you have a class?

JORDAN: So?

MAX: SO? Don't you think you should *go* to class?

JORDAN: *(Like a little kid.)* Well, gee, Mom, I kinda don't feel so good, so if ya don't mind, I'm gonna stay home today.

MAX: You look fine to me.

JORDAN: Well I don't feel fine. Hey — why don't you mind your own business?

MAX: You're supposed to be my role model.

JORDAN: I musta missed that part when I read the rule book.

MAX: You're the older brother! You're supposed to set a good example!

JORDAN: Well here's an example for you — a growing boy needs his rest. Now would you *please* shut up and let me get some sleep?!

MAX: I guess you had a rough night, huh?

JORDAN: Oh I had a great night. It was just a long night.

MAX: And you must have been drinking?

JORDAN: Why are you interrogating me?

MAX: *(Calmly — not judgmental.)* Well what kind of an example are you setting for me? You go out every night partying with your friends; you miss class all the time; you're never gonna graduate from college. You're never gonna get a good job and move away from home. You're a bum. And you're supposed to . . . ya know . . . inspire me and make me want to go to college and make something of my life. But you're not doing a very good job, and I'm worried about how *I'm* gonna turn out.

JORDAN: You're crazy, ya know that? Where did you get this idea that I'm supposed to be some perfect big brother that you look up to and try to be like . . . you're acting like this is some sort of movie: "Big brother inspires little brother to give up crack and pursue his dreams. Little Brother learns how to succeed and goes on to become a billionaire donating half his money to a foundation named after his dead older brother who died saving his little brother's life."

MAX: Hey . . . I *never* smoked crack. But that actually sounds like a pretty good movie.

JORDAN: Soap opera, ya mean.

MAX: But you've got a good imagination. You could be a writer if you ever went to school.

JORDAN: Give me a break, will you?

MAX: I'm serious, Jor. I'm worried about you.

JORDAN: Worry about yourself, OK? I'm fine. I haven't missed *that* many classes. I'm not flunking out no matter what you think. I just need to sleep in today. I've got a raging headache and you're yakking at me at 7 AM is *not* helping!

MAX: What's your GPA?

JORDAN: Oh come on . . .

MAX: I'm serious. What's your GPA right now?

JORDAN: I have no idea. Probably somewhere around . . . I don't know . . . 2.0?

MAX: 2.0! That's the lowest C possible!

JORDAN: So? It's passing. I'm passing . . .

MAX: I guess if you're satisfied with *that* . . . you must have some pretty low standards . . .

JORDAN: OK, look . . . if I promise to go to class tomorrow

and bring up my 2.0 to something a little more respectable . . . will you promise to leave this room right now and let me get some sleep?

MAX: Will you promise to keep your promise?

JORDAN: YES! I promise! I swear! I'm begging you!

MAX: Looks like maybe *I'm* the one inspiring you!

JORDAN: Yeah . . . look at that. What a strange twist of fate.

MAX: "Strange twist of fate." See, that's good — you *should* be a writer!

JORDAN: And you should go eat some breakfast and run off to school like a good little role model.

MAX: And you'll go to class tomorrow?

JORDAN: *(Rolling over and pulling the covers over his head.)* Yes, I'll go to class and I'll bring up my 2.0 and I'll be a writer.

MAX: *(Quite satisfied.)* Good. Now that's what I'm talking about!! Now I'll have some footsteps to follow in.

JORDAN: You're something else, kid! But pretty persuasive.

MAX: Yeah. I think I'm gonna be a lawyer!

JORDAN: That figures!

(MAX exits the room as JORDAN goes back to sleep.)

END OF SCENE

BUSTED

KENNY has been caught scalping concert tickets by the principal and has been given a one-week suspension. He thinks he was set up by another student and discusses the situation with his friend PAUL.

KENNY: I'm dead. I'm screwed. My life is over.

PAUL: It's only a week.

KENNY: *Only* a week! I don't care if it's only a day. My parents are going to kill me.

PAUL: I wonder if there's any way to avoid telling them why you got suspended.

KENNY: No chance. Lard Ass is sending home a letter. And he's sending it through the mail in case I "accidentally forget" to give it to them.

PAUL: You were really cool not to rat me out too.

KENNY: I think he might know that you were there, but he has no proof and of course I'd never say anything, so you're cool. I'm the jerk who got caught red-handed.

PAUL: Well — look on the bright side, no school for a week.

KENNY: You think this is gonna be some sweet vacation? You obviously don't know my parents very well. They'll make me work harder than if I *were* in class. Schoolwork. Yardwork. Clean my room. Clean the garage. They definitely believe in discipline. I told you — I'm screwed.

PAUL: Hey, man, I'm really sorry. If I got suspended for a week, my mom would say something like, "Don't eat all the food in the fridge before I get home," or something lame like that. She wouldn't even care.

KENNY: Since you're gonna be here, find out who the fink was, OK?

PAUL: What do you mean?

KENNY: You think old Lard Ass just happened to come strolling by at the exact time this deal was going down? We both know he *never* leaves his office if he doesn't have to. It was way too convenient that he caught me. Good thing he's so fat and walks so slow — two minutes sooner and he would have caught you too!

PAUL: Wow! I never thought of that. Who do you think it was?

KENNY: Don't know. Maybe Cara Williams, the little snitch. She rats out everybody. Probably thinks it looks good on her record.

PAUL: She doesn't know anything about it. It can't be her. *(Thinks for a moment.)* Hey! Maybe it's Charlie.

KENNY: Charlie? Charlie Brewer?

PAUL: Yeah. Trying to cut in on your action — gets you out of the way and he moves in.

KENNY: Charlie Brewer sells dope! I don't sell dope. I'm scalping concert tickets, for cryin' out loud! Doesn't he know that? We have two completely different types of clientele.

PAUL: Well, I'll ask around. See if I can find out anything. But I still wouldn't put it past Brewer.

KENNY: *(Shrugs.)* Anyway . . . I better get home. Can't put it off any longer.

PAUL: Ya know, you'd think your parents would be pleased.

KENNY: Pleased? Why would they be pleased? My mother's *only* dream is for me to get into an Ivy League school. She obviously has no life.

PAUL: I just mean that you're such a great businessman. I swear someday you're gonna be a millionaire.

KENNY: Yeah, right. Only if I don't flunk outta here first.

PAUL: Hey — are you holding any tickets now?

KENNY: Nah. Lardo took everything. Watch him give 'em away to some honor role boneheads and make like he's all hip and stuff — what a jerk! Why? Do you need somethin' special?

PAUL: I was just thinking I could take over . . . until you got back.

KENNY: Sorry man, but I got nothin'. Maybe I'll teach you the business when I get back from my "vacation." I'm gonna have to be real careful — they're gonna be watching me and you'd be a great cover.

PAUL: Really? Awesome! I definitely need to make some cash.

KENNY: We'll see how it goes — no promises OK?

PAUL: Yeah, sure. I understand.

KENNY: OK, I'm outta here. Call me if you hear anything.

PAUL: Will do. Take it easy — don't let the parents get to ya.

KENNY: Fat chance of that! I'm spending my week doing hard labor and that's the truth! *(KENNY exits.)*

END OF SCENE

FIGHTING THE GOOD FIGHT

CORY *is a large boy and sometimes doesn't know his own strength. His friend, SHAWN, is smaller and always seems to be on the receiving end of CORY'S physical abuse. SHAWN becomes fed up and finally confronts CORY.*

CORY *comes up behind SHAWN and swipes him across the head for no apparent reason.*

SHAWN: *(Surprised and annoyed.)* Ow! *(Turning around and seeing CORY.)* Man, I should have known it was you. What the hell did you do that for?

CORY: *(Oblivious.)* Do what?

SHAWN: What are you doing, smacking me across the head like that? That hurt man. God — you're *always* doing crap like that.

CORY: *(Laughing.)* Whatever, dude.

SHAWN: No man, not *whatever*. I'm sick of it. Keep your big paws offa me, OK? It's enough already.

CORY: Awwww . . . ittle bitty baby gonna go cryin' to Mama?

SHAWN: No Cory, I'm not cryin' to anybody. I'm not running away from you, I'm just telling you to knock it off. Stop hitting me all the time — I'm not your personal punching bag.

CORY: Chill, man . . . I didn't even know I did it. What's the big deal?

SHAWN: The big deal is that you do it all the time and you *never* know you're doing it. So I'm pointing it out to you. You're constantly going around swacking me all the damn time. Makes me wonder why you have to constantly have physical contact with me. What are you, queer or something?

CORY: Hey . . . don't *even* go there, man, or I really will beat the crap outta you.

SHAWN: You do it all the time anyway. You do it to a lot of

kids — anyone who's smaller than you. Must make you feel like a real big man.

CORY: What are you talkin' about? You make me sound like I'm some jacked-up bully or something. That is *so* not my style, dude.

SHAWN: See this bruise? Ya know how I got it? You pushed me in the hall the other day and slammed me into the lockers. Everyone was cracking up — I thought you broke my arm. Look at this one — on my knee — remember the other day I was on my board — you stuck your foot out just as I was going off the curb and totally tripped me up. I came down hard . . . it's amazing that my kneecap didn't bust wide open. Pick any kid in school under five foot three and I guarantee they'll have some sort of bruise from Sasquatch.

CORY: Who's Sasquatch?

SHAWN: My God, Cory, you really are a dope sometimes.

CORY: Shut up! I am not. Who's Sasquatch?

SHAWN: *You* — stupid! You're big and dumb and you don't even know the damage that you cause to other people.

CORY: I'm not stupid.

SHAWN: If you don't want people to think you're a bully — quit acting like one. Quit beating up on people.

CORY: We could make this even, ya know?

SHAWN: What are you talking about?

CORY: If you think I'm always beating up on you — beat up on me.

SHAWN: Yeah, right. That's a fair fight.

CORY: C'mon, man. Come at me. It'll make you feel better.

SHAWN: No, it won't. It won't make me feel better. And besides, I don't want hit you. I don't want to hit anyone. I'm a pacifist.

CORY: Use your fist. That's fine.

SHAWN: *(Exasperated.)* That's not what I . . . oh . . . what's the point? Cory — look it, I just want you to stop and think before you start swinging your arms around. In case you haven't noticed, you're a big guy and you don't even realize how strong you are. Even if you are just giving me or anyone else a friendly pat or the back — it hurts! I don't want to fight you — I just want you to stop putting bruises all over me!

CORY: I still think you'd feel better if you got all this anger out of your system. C'mon, man — hit me! *(Playfully.)* Hit me! I dare ya!

SHAWN: I told you — I'm not gonna hit you.

CORY: I won't hit ya back. This'll be a freebie. C'mon — don't be a wuss! Hit me!

SHAWN: Ya know what, Cory? I don't need to hit you. I don't care if you think I'm a wuss, but I'm walking away from this.

CORY: Why? I promise I won't fight back. It'll do you good. Build your confidence.

SHAWN: I don't need to use my fists to build my confidence, man — I use my *brain*.

CORY: Suit yourself. But it's too bad, little buddy. This would have been the opportunity of a lifetime.

SHAWN: Oh really? Hitting you would have been the opportunity of a lifetime? Well, shucks, I'm just gonna have to take my chances and hope something better comes along.

CORY: I'll try not ta bust you up anymore, buddy. I don't mean it, ya know? I'm no bully.

SHAWN: Yeah. I know. Who knows? Maybe someday when I'm rich and famous I'll hire you to be my bodyguard.

CORY: Awesome! That would be like the coolest. Thanks, man! You're the best —

(He starts to hit SHAWN across the back — SHAWN is able to stop him just in the nick of time.)

SHAWN: Hey! Hey! Take it easy — no more hitting, remember?

CORY: Oh right. Whoops — sorry dude — I already forgot!

SHAWN: I know. I know. We're really gonna have to work on this!

END OF SCENE

PRETTY PICTURES

RYAN shows BOBBY a copy of a Playboy *magazine that he stole from his father's collection. After admiring some of the photos, BOBBY gets a big shock when he actually recognizes one of the models.*

RYAN: Check it out bro. I scored!

BOBBY: What is it? *(Sees the cover of the magazine.)* Oh, man! Is that what I think it is?

RYAN: Yup! Have you ever seen pictures like this? They're unbelievable.

BOBBY: Of course! I've seen *Playboy* a million times — the girls are very *very* hot.

RYAN: A million times? I don't think so. I don't think you've ever seen a naked girl in your life.

BOBBY: I have too.

RYAN: When?

BOBBY: I don't know when exactly. I don't keep a record of every naked woman I've seen. *(Thinks for a minute.)* Titanic! The girl was naked in *Titanic*. I watched that movie like a trillion times. We own the DVD! If I need to see a naked woman in the middle of the night, I can just pop in that movie. She is totally awesome.

RYAN: Oh yeah. That scene was great. She's lying there all naked. But check this out. The girls in here are incredible. Let me show you my future wife. *(He flips to the centerfold.)*

BOBBY: Whoa! She's . . . really . . . . uh . . . *tan.*

RYAN: Dude! You're turning all red. I can't believe it — you're actually blushing.

BOBBY: Well . . . she's the kind of girl who makes a man weak in the knees.

RYAN: You got that right. Let me show you this layout. They

did this photo shoot of a bunch of college girls. Really smart girls with really hot bods.

BOBBY: College girls, huh? Not real models?

RYAN: No, they're not models, but check them out. They're totally hot. And they go to like Harvard and Yale and stuff. Can you imagine being that good-looking *and* having brains?

BOBBY: Let me see that. *(He grabs the magazine from RYAN and starts looking through it.)*

RYAN: Hey take it easy, man. Don't rip it — my dad would have a cow. I've gotta get it back before he realizes I took it. He doesn't think I know where he keeps them and I think it's better that way. If he knew I *knew* where they were, he'd hide 'em so I'd never find them. Gotta have my naked-girl fix.

BOBBY: *(Abruptly closes the magazine and lets it drop to the ground.)* I think I'm gonna be sick.

RYAN: *(Picking up the magazine and smoothing it out.)* Hey, I just told you not to mess it around with this. What are you throwing it on the ground for?

BOBBY: I'm not kidding — I'm think I'm going to puke.

RYAN: Why? Looking at all that gorgeous flesh makes you want to vomit? What's up with that?

BOBBY: Look at page 102.

RYAN: *(Turning to it.)* Your future wife?

BOBBY: Not even!

RYAN: *(Sees the photo.)* Nice taste buddy. She's a beauty!

BOBBY: *(Numb.)* Look at her name.

RYAN: Let's see . . . uh . . . oh, here it is . . . the beautiful Melissa.

BOBBY: Look where she goes to school.

RYAN: Says here she goes to . . . Princeton — majoring in economics! Smart girl. She's gonna be rich some day too! Nice combination. Beauty and bucks!

BOBBY: Stop looking at her boobs and look at her face for a second!

RYAN: Yeah man . . . like I said . . . she's a beaut . . . Wait a minute! Oh, my God! Is this? This couldn't be . . . this isn't your . . .

BOBBY: It is Ryan! It's my *sister*! My sister . . . Melissa. Who goes to Princeton. And is making my dad so proud by being an econ major. Now do you see why I'm gonna be sick.

RYAN: She is so hot! I didn't remember how hot she was.

BOBBY: *Ryan!* That's my sister, for crying out loud!

RYAN: Well . . . now you know how she's paying her college tuition.

BOBBY: My parents are paying. She doesn't need to do that to pay for school.

RYAN: Girl's gotta have some spending dough.

BOBBY: You're not being very understanding!

RYAN: Bobby, c'mon. Stop getting your shorts all twisted for nothing. What's the big deal? She's great-looking. They probably paid her a ton of dough — why shouldn't she do it?

BOBBY: Because she's naked for all the world to see!! And she has a little brother with perverted friends! And what's gonna happen when my *dad* sees this? He's gonna have a heart attack. He'll have a heart attack and drop dead! She's going to kill my father!

RYAN: *(Looking at the photo again.)* I think you're overreacting.

BOBBY: *(Grabbing the magazine from him.)* Will you stop looking at that!

RYAN: What are ya gonna do, man? Buy up every copy and stop all the men in the world from looking at your sis? Let it go. She obviously doesn't care if people see her . . . in all her beautiful glory.

BOBBY: Don't say a word of this to anyone. Don't show anyone else that magazine. Put it back where it came from. I'm gonna call Mel and ask her what the heck was she thinking?

RYAN: My dad's gonna see it. My dad's gonna see it and lust after your sister.

BOBBY: I know. Now do you understand why I feel sick?

RYAN: What if my dad tells your dad that he saw her?

BOBBY: Oh, God. That can't happen. I gotta call her right now. Why would she *do* this? Later.
(*BOBBY runs off distractedly.*)
RYAN: (*Opening the magazine again and looking at the photo of Melissa.*) Hell-ooooo, Melissa! Forget that centerfold — I'm thinking *you* are now my future wife!

 END OF SCENE

AND THE BAND PLAYED ON

ADAM has the difficult task of telling BRET that they've decided to replace him as the lead singer in the band that BRET started.

BRET: Hey, man, what was it you wanted to talk to me about? But make it quick cause I gotta get going pretty soon.

ADAM: If you don't have the time right now, then let's talk later — this is important and it may take a while.

BRET: Cryptic! What's going on?

ADAM: Maybe we should wait for T.J. and Luke before getting into all of it.

BRET: Oh, it's about the band? You get us a gig finally?

ADAM: Yeah it's about the band and *no* — no gig . . . *yet.* I'm working on it, though.

BRET: Excellent — keep it up! OK, I gotta motor.
(He starts to leave and ADAM calls after him.)

ADAM: Hold up! I still have to talk to you about something.

BRET: Well spill it, dude, I'm a busy man.

ADAM: *(Reluctantly — this is difficult for him to say.)* Well, that's kinda what I wanted to talk to you about. The guys and I noticed that you're really busy . . . *all the time!* Lot's going on . . . that's cool and everything . . . but, the thing is . . . you rarely make it to rehearsals and if you do come, you usually leave early and it's very hard to get a gig when you haven't learned half the songs we do.

BRET: *(Annoyed.)* It's my frickin' band!

ADAM: First of all, it's not *your* band. Maybe it was your idea to start the thing, and *yes*, you're the front man . . . but it's not *your* band, Bret . . . it's *our* band. And the only way we can be successful is if everyone carries their own weight. Being the lead singer doesn't give you the right to show up whenever you please.

BRET: I carry my weight! This band would have never existed if it hadn't been for me. I do what it takes to make it work.

ADAM: *What!?* What do you do? Hit on girls constantly to make yourself feel like a rock star? Yeah, you do that really well.

BRET: You said it yourself — I'm the front man. Without me, this band would fall apart in two seconds.

ADAM: Actually we've been playing without you and we seem to be doing just fine. Since you're constantly blowing off rehearsals we asked Clark Williams to sit in a couple of times and he was . . .

(BRET is furious at the mention of Clark's name and interrupts.)

BRET: Clark Williams?! Are you *kidding* me? That kid couldn't play a note if his life depended on it!

ADAM: He didn't play. He sang . . . and his voice . . . well, let me tell ya . . . his voice is off the hook!

BRET: I'm the lead singer and I don't need anyone to back me up vocally! Get rid of him — we don't need him.

ADAM: The truth is, Bret, we *do* need him. 'Cause you're never there. And he's fantastic. I've been trying to talk to you about this for a while, man, and you keep dodging me. It seems pretty clear, doesn't it? If the band is gonna survive, if we really are serious about this and want to start booking gigs, we've all decided that the best thing to do is bring in Clark and let you go.

BRET: *(Stunned and furious.)* Replacing me with Clark Williams? That's what you think would be best? This is mutiny! You're kicking me out of my own band? The band I started? I brought every single one of you guys into it — it was my idea! You can't do this to me!

ADAM: It stopped being your band a long time ago. I'm sorry, man, I really am. But you seem to have too much other stuff going on and you don't really seem to care about it anymore. Don't take it personally.

BRET: How can I *not* take it personally? You've basically told me to my face that I suck!

ADAM: If you'd just started showing up to rehearsals this wouldn't have to happen. I mean, we've written three new songs that you've never even heard.

BRET: Fine. You want Clark Williams to ruin the band? Fine. I don't need this bull. There's plenty of other guys who'd love to be in a band with me.

ADAM: I'm sure there are.

BRET: Good. Who needs it? And who needs you traitors? You guys can all go to hell.

ADAM: Interesting that you just said that, 'cause that's what we're thinking of naming the band.

BRET: What are you talking about?

ADAM: Our new name for the band — "Going to Hell." Cool, right?

BRET: *(Disgusted.)* Oh that's just *too* perfect!

END OF SCENE

LICENSED TO DRIVE?

BRYAN has just flunked his driving test, but it is extremely important that he be able to drive for his upcoming date. Here, he asks his older brother ALEX to help him out with his problem.

ALEX: Hey, hey, hey — here he is: the licensed driver. It's official, right?

BRYAN: 'Fraid not.

ALEX: What are you talking about?

BRYAN: I'm not licensed. It's not official. I didn't pass the stupid test.

ALEX: You've gotta be kidding?

BRYAN: Do I look like I'm kidding? I didn't pass, OK? Don't make a big deal about it.

ALEX: So . . . uh . . . how come? I mean do you know what you did wrong?

BRYAN: The guy was a jerk, ya know? He had it in for me before I even started the car. I think he must get off on flunking people.

ALEX: So you were fine? It was just the guy that was a jerk?

BRYAN: Well, *because* he was a jerk, he made me nervous. I guess I kinda went right through a stop sign. I guess that's like an "automatic failure" or something. Big deal! I didn't hit anybody or anything.

ALEX: *(Obviously amused.)* Well, I'm sorry, Bry. I know you were looking forward to getting the thing. But you can take it again — just make sure you get another person to give you the test. And make sure you stop when you're supposed to.

BRYAN: You passed your first time.

ALEX: I got lucky; I had a woman examiner. I think she was hot for me.

BRYAN: Shut up! You think all woman are hot for you . . .

ALEX: Well I got all the looks in this family — you know it's true!

BRYAN: Speaking of women . . .

ALEX: Yeah? What about 'em? You need lessons in that department?

BRYAN: What I need is a license. To drive. So I can pick Becky up for our date.

ALEX: You have a date! Wow man — you really are moving up in the world. So who's Becky?

BRYAN: She's a girl who agreed to go out with me because she thought *I could drive!*

ALEX: Ohhhh . . . you've got a problem.

BRYAN: Can you help?

ALEX: What do you want me to do? Drive you on your date? That's not cool.

BRYAN: I really like this girl and I don't want to blow it. What are we supposed to do — take the bus? I was counting on having my license for Friday night and Mom already told me I could use the car *if* I passed — and then we just laughed because we both knew I would pass. That guy at the DMV has ruined my life!

ALEX: Suck it up, bro. Just call her and tell her what happened. She'll understand.

BRYAN: Maybe. But she'll also cancel. 'Cause she made a big deal about how much she hates being driven around and she can't wait to get her license and she hates going out with guys who don't drive.

ALEX: Sounds like a real catch.

BRYAN: Yeah — kinda high maintenance, right?

ALEX: You said it! Look, if she won't go out with you because you flunked your driving test, is she really the kind of girl you want to be with anyway?

BRYAN: I didn't inherit your looks, remember? Not too many girls ever say yes to going out with me. So when one finally does, I feel like I'd better take advantage of the situation, ya know what I mean?

ALEX: So what do you want me to do?

BRYAN: Let me use your car.

ALEX: You're out of your mind!

BRYAN: Come on. I *know* how to drive. I'm a good driver. It's perfectly safe to get in the car with me. I just need a car to get over there, pick up Becky, go to the movies, and then go home. See — it's not even a lot of driving around. All surface streets. No one will ever have to know but me and you.

ALEX: You'll never get away with it.

BRYAN: I will if you help me. Mom and Dad will never find out if *you* don't tell them.

ALEX: And if *you* don't get pulled over.

BRYAN: I'll only get pulled over if I do something wrong. And I'm not gonna do anything wrong. I'll be the most perfect driver in the world — maintain speed limit, wear my seat belt, hands at ten o'clock and two o'clock. I *know* what to do. Please help me out. I'd do it for you. That's what brothers are for.

ALEX: Oh, now here comes the guilt trip. Well . . . I totally understand your predicament, man, but God — if anything should happen — an accident or anything — we would both be so screwed!!

BRYAN: Nothing's gonna happen.

ALEX: You can't control that. You don't know that. What if you're driving perfectly and someone rear-ends you. Not your fault — but now you're in big trouble cause you gotta exchange info — insurance, driver's license — ya know? It could happen.

BRYAN: So give me your license. It's not gonna happen, but just in case — I'll give 'em your info and we can always say it was you who was driving.

ALEX: You have a criminal mind. I never knew this about you.

BRYAN: I want this girl to like me!! Just this once — and I'll never ask you for anything ever again.

ALEX: I don't know, man. This is big time.

BRYAN: I will be incredibly careful. And if anything should happen, which it won't, but if anything does happen, I promise to take full responsibility for it.

ALEX: How are you planning to carry this out without Mom and Dad finding out?

BRYAN: You park your car down the street. I say I'm going to study over at Eddie's. You say you're goin' out — they never ask you where you're going anymore anyway — it's all covered. I'm back by eleven and park the car down the block. Walk home — it's all good!

ALEX: You scare me.

BRYAN: Cut it out — what do you say? Is it a deal?

ALEX: I must be crazy, but yeah — I'll do it. But I swear, if anything happens, I will kill you so hard!

BRYAN: Relax! Nothing will go wrong. It'll be perfect. And next week I'll take the test again and get my own license for real.

ALEX: Let's hope so.

BRYAN: Have faith, bro.

ALEX: Believe me, I'm gonna be praying all night long!

END OF SCENE

TWO-TIMER

NATHAN and BEN discover they have both made a date with the same girl for the same night. They realized this girl has duped them and they decide how they would like to get even with her.

NATHAN: I didn't *bribe* her — what are you talking about? I asked her out and she said yes — that's it! That's the whole situation.

BEN: Why would she say yes to you when she agreed to go out with me?

NATHAN: You'd have to ask her that. All I know is that I did get a date with Lucy for Friday night, and I'm taking her out.

BEN: Not without a fight on your hands, man. We both know Lucy agreed to go out with me first.

NATHAN: Are you sure you got the date right? Are you sure it's *this* Friday?

BEN: I'm not an idiot, Nathan. It's this Friday and I asked her last week. You asked her yesterday. I've got priority.

NATHAN: Seniority.

BEN: Whatever. It's *my* date.

NATHAN: Maybe she's the one who got it mixed up. I mean, why would she make two dates for the same night?

BEN: What time were you supposed to pick her up?

NATHAN: Late. She said it was the only time she could get away from her family. She had some big family thing she had to do first. But it was cool since she had a late curfew — being Friday and all.

BEN: How late?

NATHAN: Nine thirty. We're gonna go to a late movie. Why? What time did she tell you?

BEN: Five o'clock. She said she had to make it early because she needed to be home by nine for some family meeting.

NATHAN: What is going on? What's with this girl?

BEN: Two-timed us, bro. We are the victims! I can't believe it. She stacked the deck — two dates in one night.

NATHAN: And she's cutting it pretty close too. Home from the first date by nine, the next guy picks up by nine thirty — what a little ho.

BEN: Did she think we wouldn't find out?

NATHAN: Lucy — perfect name for a girl like that. Loose — e! Skanky is more like it!

BEN: Sorry, man. I was ready to get into it with you over this girl. Boy, do I feel stupid.

NATHAN: I know. Me too. Well, we can't let her get away with it.

BEN: No way!

NATHAN: I wonder how many other guys she's done this to.

BEN: The thing is — she lied to our face. I mean, if she had said to me "I need to get home early cause I'm catchin' a movie with Nathan later," I don't think I'd mind so much. But she made up these stories about having to be with her family — that totally stinks!

NATHAN: I don't know — it would be bad anyway you look at it.

BEN: So what should we do? Write B-I-T-C-H on her locker?

NATHAN: No! We need to handle it more adultlike.

BEN: So what do you want to do?

NATHAN: The only thing we can do, man — stand her up!

BEN: Stand her up?

NATHAN: A no-show. She's waiting for you to pick her up at five. You don't show up. Maybe she tries to call you and can't get a hold of you. "Oh well," she thinks, "the night's not totally wasted. Nathan will be here at nine thirty." Then I don't show up! Revenge is sweet!

BEN: *Or* we both show up at nine thirty. She opens her door and we're both there, standing on her doorstep. She knows we've caught her red-handed.

NATHAN: That's it! That's definitely what we have to do. We

won't say a word. It'll just be the two of us standing at her front door. Staring her down. She'll be totally humiliated.

BEN: Fo' sure man!

NATHAN: And we won't ever let some girl make fools of us again, right?

BEN: No way!

NATHAN: And afterwards, maybe the two of us can go get something to eat?

BEN: Yeah and maybe we'll pick up a couple of nice girls. One for each of us. No more two-timers.

NATHAN: Hey — that sounds like a great idea to me! Let's do it!

(They shake hands.)

END OF SCENE

SAVED BY A FRIEND

GABE comes upon CHARLIE who is surrounded by books and papers strewn about. He is trying to stuff everything frantically into his backpack. In helping CHARLIE pick up his things, GABE comes to find out that what CHARLIE really needs is a friend.

GABE: Hey bud — what happened? Looks like your locker exploded.

CHARLIE: Just leave me alone.

GABE: I'm tryin' to help you, man. Your stuff is everywhere. What happened?

CHARLIE: Just a typical day at Washington High.

GABE: *(Helping him pick up his things.)* What do you mean?

CHARLIE: I mean this happens every damn day. I get jumped; I get knocked over. "Hey, let's have some fun and pull apart Charlie's backpack — dump all his stuff all over the place." These guys need to get a life.

GABE: Who's doing this to you?

CHARLIE: You've gotta be kidding . . . you can't figure it out? Besides, I know when to keep my mouth shut. It's bad enough without having them think I'm some sort of rat.

GABE: I guess I do know who you're talking about. Those guys are major jerks.

CHARLIE: Tell me about it. Hey, thanks for helping me pick this stuff up.

GABE: No problem. Are you taking all this stuff home with you?

CHARLIE: Yeah.

GABE: But it's Friday! Why are you taking every single book you own home for the weekend?

CHARLIE: Um . . . I've got a lot of catching up to do.

GABE: What did you say your name was?

CHARLIE: I didn't.

GABE: Well . . . what's your name, man?

CHARLIE: It's Charlie. Look, thanks for your help, but I really . . .

GABE: Charlie, hold up! You're telling me your spending the entire weekend studying? Man, you've got to lighten up. Have a little fun. Where do you live?

CHARLIE: Why do you want to know? What am I, your good deed for the day?

GABE: No . . . it's just . . . I know what it's like to be picked on. Used to happen to me all the time. My first year at this school I was a real loner. And just like you, I got jumped practically every day. But eventually I made some friends and I guess I got some confidence — eventually I stopped getting hassled by those morons. All I'm saying is that I know where you're at . . . and I'd like to help if I can.

CHARLIE: *(Blurting out all his frustration.)* I hate it here. I can't take it anymore. Every day it's the same thing and I'm losin' it. My parents have no idea how bad it is. Teachers don't know . . . or care. The truth is I'm taking all these books home because I don't plan on coming back. I'm checkin' out. I've had enough.

GABE: Checking out of this school?

CHARLIE: Out of life, man! I don't mean I just hate it here at school — I hate it *here!* Planet Earth. I want out!

GABE: *(Shaken, but understanding.)* Charlie, man — c'mon . . . it's gonna get better. I mean, I don't even know you, but I do know what you're going through, I swear I do. I *was* you two years ago. I met some people — some good people to help me get through it and now I'm able to help you if you let me.

CHARLIE: I don't get why you'd want to? Like you said, you don't even know me. I don't even know your name. Why would you want to help a total stranger?

GABE: My name's Gabe. And I want to help you because I'm trying to . . . I don't know — give back — pay it forward — whatever you want to call it. I got help and now

I can give help. You need a friend, Charlie. Who do you ever talk to about this stuff?

CHARLIE: No one. I guess that's why I'm spilling my guts to a stranger. It's all pent up inside me.

GABE: What do you say we put some of these books back in your locker and then go grab a frappuccino or something.

CHARLIE: I don't know.

GABE: C'mon, Charlie — I'm buying. Ya know a bunch of my friends are getting together tomorrow to play a little football. Why don't you join us?

CHARLIE: That actually sounds cool. I'm not a very good player though.

GABE: Doesn't matter, neither are we. Now let's get outta here — it's the weekend man, time to relax.

CHARLIE: Gabe . . . I still don't get why you're being so nice to me . . . but thanks! Thanks a lot. I appreciate what you're tryin' to do.

GABE: Hey . . . you can never have too many friends, ya know? It's what helps you get through the bad times.

CHARLIE: Well these are really bad times, Gabe. I don't think a football game with the guys is gonna help me much.

GABE: Well, ya never know. It might help you more than you realize. But let's just take one thing at a time. And right now I could really use some caffeine and sugar. So let's go. And we can talk or not — whatever you want. But the thing that helped me the most was realizing I wasn't alone. Now you don't have to be either.

CHARLIE: Well . . . I guess I really didn't feel like lugging all those books home anyway.

GABE: That's what I'm talking about! They'll be here waiting for you when you come back on Monday.

CHARLIE: When I come back?

GABE: Yeah Charlie. I have every reason to believe you'll be back here Monday morning. And I have a feeling things will be a lot different by then.

CHARLIE: Things don't change overnight. Or over a weekend.

GABE: No. But take it slow. And now that you've made a friend . . . maybe things won't seem so bleak.

CHARLIE: You're cool, man. And who knows? You might be saving my life.

GABE: Good! I think it's a life worth saving! Now let's go get that drink!

END OF SCENE

HOT SOUNDS

DIMITRI is an employee at a very large electronics store. He has recently acquired a new sound system and is eager to show it off to his friend WILLIE. WILLIE, however, learns that DIMITRI did not obtain this new stereo with his employee discount — but by taking advantage of his position and stealing the equipment.

DIMITRI: Check it out! It's top-of-the-line, state-of-the-art equipment. The best money can buy!

WILLIE: So where'd *you* get the money to buy it?

DIMITRI: Didn't need it, man. I've got connections.

WILLIE: You're standing there telling me that you now own the best sound system known to man and you didn't shell out one single dime?

DIMITRI: Well, it's who ya know . . .

WILLIE: What's with all the mystery? Tell me how you got all this stuff.

DIMITRI: Well as you know, I'm the top salesman at Electronic World.

WILLIE: So? They're not in the habit of just giving away their merchandise to employees, are they?

DIMITRI: I never said anyone "gave" it to me.

WILLIE: Did you win it or something? Like the salesman who sells the most TVs wins a sound system?

DIMITRI: That'll work.

WILLIE: What's that supposed to mean?

DIMITRI: It means that sounds like a believable story. I think I'll use that one.

WILLIE: But that's *not* how you got it . . .

DIMITRI: Well . . . that's what I'll tell the folks anyway.

WILLIE: Dimitri . . . did you rip 'em off? Is that what you're saying? Did you actually steal all this?

DIMITRI: Man, you wouldn't believe how easy it is to take stuff from that place. There's nobody there at night except me and a couple of other really cool guys. The manager *always* leaves early 'cause he's hot for some chick who works across the street, so he always leaves when she does. The other guys don't care who takes what.

WILLIE: What about the inventory? Don't they do inventory? Aren't they going to notice that something as big and expensive as this is missing?

DIMITRI: I guess . . . I'm not too worried about it.

WILLIE: You're an imbecile. They're totally going to find out and when they do, they're gonna track it to you.

DIMITRI: Even if they do find out some stuff is missing, they'll never find out it's me. There's no proof.

WILLIE: The proof's sitting right here, you moron!

DIMITRI: You think they're gonna come to my house and search my room? I don't think so. It's not gonna get that far. Besides, it's no loss for them. They just, ya know, write it off or something. Nobody's getting hurt. It's no big deal.

WILLIE: Do you know that every time someone steals something from a store, that gives them an excuse to jack up the prices to cover their loss. You're ruining it for everyone, man.

DIMITRI: *(Sarcastically.)* Gee Officer Willie. I'm sorry. I'll bring it back like a good little boy. Give me a break!

WILLIE: Other people are doing this too?

DIMITRI: One other guy I know of. But probably everyone's taken something at some point. It's too easy.

WILLIE: It's stealing! Large, expensive equipment. You're gonna get caught. And you're gonna get fired. And then you're gonna go to jail.

DIMITRI: I'm gonna get away with it. Hey, what's with you anyhow? I thought you'd be stoked about it. I could probably set you up with the same system. Bet that'll make you change your tune, right? Of course . . . I need to wait awhile. I can't take two of these babies in the same week. *See* . . . I am cautious!

WILLIE: You are wack, you know that? You are totally, totally wack. Don't do me any favors. Don't go bringing me a hot stereo. I don't want it. I don't want anything to do with it.

DIMITRI: *(Turning up the volume on the stereo.)* Ahhhh . . . just listen to that bass.

WILLIE: Don't give me your sales pitch. I'm not going there. This is all gonna catch up to you one day man and bite you hard in the ass.

DIMITRI: Maybe. I doubt it though. I'm not working there forever. I'll be long gone before they even notice. Just tell me if you change your mind though, bro, and I'll hook you up. Oh, and by the way, you *will* be keepin' all this information on the down low, right? I don't have to worry about that, do I?

WILLIE: You think I'd turn you in? It might do you some good.

DIMITRI: Dude! What are you all of a sudden? My conscience?

WILLIE: You certainly could use one!

END OF SCENE

PERFORMANCE ENHANCEMENT

ANDREW runs track and has a big race coming up with a highly competitive opponent from a rival school. His friend DAVID thinks the only way to win would be to take steroids or some type of performance-enhancement drug. Here, he tries to convince ANDREW it's his only way to success.

DAVID: I don't have to tell you how fast that guy from Lincoln is. If you don't take some sort of action, he's gonna leave you in the dust and then where will you be?

ANDREW: What do you mean, "take some sort of action"? I'm training for this meet as hard as I can. I want to go on to the state finals just as much as the next guy, but if he's better than me, he's better than me . . . there's only so much I can do about it.

DAVID: Don't be a jerk. You're giving up too easily! There's plenty you can do.

ANDREW: You're acting as if I can become the bionic man over night.

DAVID: You can. You know you can.

ANDREW: You mean that stuff Curtis was telling us about? No thanks.

DAVID: Why? Why do you think those guys at Lincoln win every single meet? They're not a bunch of pussies — they'll do whatever it takes to win.

ANDREW: I want to win too, ya know — but I won't do drugs.

DAVID: They're not drugs. They're "performance enhancements."

ANDREW: That's just a fancy name for drugs, you airhead. Forget it! You're not selling me on this idea. Haven't you heard that college athletes are dropping dead from this crap?

DAVID: Well, you're not in college yet . . . you still have a chance!

ANDREW: Oh, that's funny. You're a real laugh riot; ya know that?

DAVID: Seriously man, they only report on the guys that die, but so many other athletes take these things and are fine. More than fine. They're *winning!* If you win this race, it would be a shoo-in for a scholarship. Probably a full ride too. Every university in the state will be fighting over you. You gotta do it, man. It's your future.

ANDREW: That's the exact reason why I won't take these "enhancements." I'd like to *have* a future. Look, I know you mean well, but I've seen what this stuff can do to people. They really mess you up, man. They're hard to get off of . . . they screw with your mind *and* body. I don't want to take the chance. It's my life we're talking about here. Not just one race — but the rest of my life!

DAVID: You're a fool. I'm sorry, but you are. One time is not gonna mess up your entire life. One time is gonna help you win and *improve* your life. Can't you see that?

ANDREW: I don't want to argue with you about this anymore. If you want to take them, go ahead — be my guest. I'm not gonna stop you. But you need to let me decide what's right for me. And I don't want to go there, OK? So please — drop the subject!

DAVID: If that guy from Lincoln is taking something and you're not, how fair will that competition be? I'm just trying to get you to even the playing field, ya know? Otherwise you literally won't have a chance in hell on Saturday.

ANDREW: Well, maybe his coach will get an anonymous tip and they'll suddenly have to do random drug testing. He'll have to forfeit and I'll win. That would be sweet.

DAVID: Dream on . . . his coach is probably the one who turned him on to that stuff in the first place.

ANDREW: All I know is that I'm gonna do my best and whatever happens . . . happens.

DAVID: That's some powerful junk you're up against. Without it — Lincoln's gonna blow you away. You might try your best, but I'm afraid your best isn't gonna be good enough.

ANDREW: It'll have to be. I'm not going to be a statistic. I don't want to be the seventeen-year-old athlete who dies from a heart attack after winning the state championships. It's not worth it, man. Even if I went out in a blaze of glory. I don't want to die at seventeen. Can't you understand that? Doesn't that make the slightest bit of sense to you?

DAVID: I think you're overreacting. You think you're gonna die and you're not. You're going to have an edge on this guy and you're going to have a better chance of winning. Doesn't *that* make sense to you?

ANDREW: OK. You see this thing your way and I see it mine. I told you, I'm not doing it. Do what you want. Take what you want. Die if you want. I'm running this race without any outside "help." May the best man win. OK? And that's all I'm gonna say about it.

END OF SCENE

ARTISTIC INTEGRITY

RAY has recently won the "best artist in the school" contest for creating an original comic book character named Dirtbag. CARLOS, however, claims that Dirtbag is his original creation and that RAY has ripped off his idea. Here, CARLOS confronts RAY about it.

CARLOS: Congratulations, man. It must be nice being the best artist in the school.

RAY: Hey, it's cool, ya know. Now everyone's asking me to do different projects and stuff for them. It's great!

CARLOS: Too bad it wasn't even your idea that won you that contest.

RAY: Huh? What's that supposed to mean?

CARLOS: It means you ripped me off, man. You stole my idea.

RAY: You're crazy.

CARLOS: Oh really? If I'm crazy, then do me a favor. Tell me how you thought of it.

RAY: Thought of what?

CARLOS: The comic book character you created for the contest — Dirtbag. How did you come up with that idea? What made you think of it?

RAY: Hey I don't have to tell you nothin'.

CARLOS: You won't tell me because you *can't* tell me. Because it's not your original idea. Dirtbag was my idea. And you stole him.

RAY: Whatever, man. That's just not true. And even if it was true, you couldn't prove it anyway.

CARLOS: I'm not gonna take away your precious title as best artist in the school. And you can keep the stinkin' fifty-dollar certificate too for all I care. But I want my character back. You saw my sketches a couple of months ago, and I know you remember. You were asking me all these questions about how I came up with the character of Dirtbag, the superhero. You even asked me if I planned on entering the contest and I told you no. You totally stole him right out from under me.

RAY: Carlos, chill out, man. Nobody stole anything from anyone. I've been working on this character for ages — maybe you helped me come up with the name, but the sketch is mine.

CARLOS: You copied him from me down to the last detail. The way his pants wrinkle, the boots, the sunglasses. Even the ring he wears . . . it's all mine!

RAY: I don't know what to tell you, man. Maybe *you* saw *my* sketches and subconsciously drew him and now you think he's yours. I've been doodling Dirtbag since as long as I can remember. And I have no memory of ever seeing you sketch a character that even slightly resembled him. You're wrong, dude. Step up and admit it.

CARLOS: I admit nothing. You're a thief and the worst kind too. Taking credit for someone else's hard work. I have Dirtbag drawings from a year ago. Signed by me! With the date on them. I wasn't going to go to the art committee, but now I think I will. Not only are you taking the praise for my work, you're so frickin' cocky about it. You're the dirt bag!

RAY: You can report me but it's not going to do any good. They'll think you're just a jealous wannabe. I won that contest fair and square. I handed my portfolio in on time. Where was your portfolio, Carlos? There's no way you can prove this character belongs to you. Signed drawings from a year ago? How can you prove that? You could have done those yesterday and put last year's date on it. That's no proof. Just let it go my friend. I *am* the best artist in this school. If you want your own comic book character, I suggest you create one — and stop saying Dirtbag is yours, because we both know the real truth.

CARLOS: Fine, Ray. I'll create a new character. I think I'll call him Ray the Rat. And when it comes time for you to develop some new material, you'll show your true colors.

There you'll be sitting in front of your empty sketchbook with absolutely nothing to show for your time. Cause you've got *no* talent! You've got to go rip off other people to make yourself look good. Ya know what? I feel sorry for you. One of these days, it's gonna catch up to you. You're gonna rip off the wrong person. And people are gonna know you for the fraud that you are.

RAY: Carlos, dude . . . you shouldn't be so bitter. You should have just entered the contest and then it would have been a fair fight. But now you're making all these accusations after the fact and you're the one who's gonna end up looking like a fool. Give it up, man.

CARLOS: *(Suddenly remembering he has something over RAY.)* Wait a minute. Did you copyright them?

RAY: Copyright what?

CARLOS: Your drawings. Dirtbag. Did you copyright him?

RAY: *(Laughing uncomfortably.)* Uh . . . no. I'm not even sure how to do that. Don't you have to go to Washington, D.C., or something? Fill out a lot of forms?

CARLOS: You think I'm gonna tell you how to do it? I've got a copyright on the comic *I* created. A year ago. It was copyrighted a year ago. Dirtbag is mine. He will always be mine and I have the copyright to prove it. You're screwed.

RAY: I think you're bluffing.

CARLOS: Really? Try me.

RAY: *(Worried for the first time.)* So what're you going to do?

CARLOS: I told you I was ready to settle this peacefully, but you're so full of yourself, I think you need to be cut down to size.

RAY: Carlos, man . . . c'mon . . . I'm sorry. We can settle this peacefully. No need to drag all those other people into it.

CARLOS: *(Laughing; he is victorious!)* I have totally got you where I want you. Now you're worried. Are you willing to admit Dirtbag is my creation?

RAY: *(Trying to maintain dignity.)* I'm willing to admit we collaborated.

CARLOS: *Ray* . . . do you want me to shame you in front of the entire school?

RAY: *(He knows he's lost the battle and completely loses his cool.)* OK. OK. He's yours. I copied him from a page I swiped out of your sketchbook about a month ago. When you said you weren't entering the contest, I thought it was my big chance. I'm sorry.

CARLOS: Don't you ever, *ever* touch my stuff again. I could sue you over this.

RAY: I'm sorry. I won't touch your stuff again. Hey, I'm even willing to give you the fifty bucks.

CARLOS: Keep it. You'll need it. You're never gonna earn another dime with your artwork.

RAY: Ya know you should be flattered. Your work is totally worth stealing.

CARLOS: Guess what, Ray? I'm not flattered. Stay away from me *and* my sketchbook. And consider yourself very lucky that I don't get you suspended for this.

RAY: Hey man, thanks. Thanks a lot. You're really decent.

CARLOS: Yeah. I am. Too bad I can't say the same about you.

END OF SCENE

Scenes for
One Female and One Male

DANCING AT THE PROM

*JOEY and JENNY are at their high school prom, but
JENNY is sitting at a table by herself. She is obviously
in an agitated state. JOEY enters uplifted and energized
as he comes off the dance floor.*

JOEY: Man, that DJ rocks! I didn't expect to dance so much —
figured it would be lame — but man, he's really good.

JENNY: *(Sarcastically.)* I'm so glad *you're* having a good time.

JOEY: What's wrong?

JENNY: What's wrong? You have to ask?

JOEY: Um . . . yeah. I'm sorry, Jen, but I thought we were both
having a good time.

JENNY: Well, I'm having *such* a great time, that I'd really like
to leave, OK?

JOEY: What? Why? We just got here. What's wrong with you?

JENNY: You are so dense!

JOEY: Thanks. I'm glad to know what you really think of me.
Could ya just clue me in on why you're freakin' out?

JENNY: I'm not freakin' out, Joey. I'm just upset. Can't you
tell when someone is upset or are you that clueless?

JOEY: It's very obvious you're upset, but honestly, Jen, I really
don't know why. I don't know what I did.

JENNY: Think about it.

JOEY: I thought I was doing everything right. I really wanted
to make you happy. *(Pause while he thinks . . . and then it
occurs to him.)* Ohhhhhh . . . are you uh . . . are you upset
because I was dancing with Julia?

JENNY: Ten years later, ladies and gentlemen, but he finally figures it out!

JOEY: I only danced with her because I thought you wanted to
take a break. You said your shoes hurt.

JENNY: My shoes do hurt. And I did want to take a break. With
you. I wanted to sit down *with you* and have something to

drink and talk to our friends. But then you suddenly become John Travolta in *Saturday Night Fever*. You can't stop dancing! *(Pause.)* And you had to dance with *her*.

JOEY: She's your best friend, why wouldn't I dance with her?

JENNY: Is that what she told you when she was whispering in your ear? That we're best friends? What a joke! The only reason she's friends with me is so she can get close to you.

JOEY: You're paranoid.

JENNY: I am not! I see the way she looks at you. I've heard her talking about you to some of the other girls. She wants you, Joey, and she's doing everything she can to make it happen. And you are completely dense if you don't see it for yourself. She's totally trying to humiliate me and you know what? It's working. I feel totally humiliated. I need to get out of here. I really want to leave.

JOEY: Jesus, Jen, there's no reason to feel humiliated. We were just dancing for crying out loud. Nothing is going on between me and Julia — you've got to get that out of your head right now! And I don't want to leave after being here for only an hour. This thing cost me a small fortune. I never wanted to come to this prom in the first place, if you remember, but since it was so important to you, we're here. You wanted a limo . . . we got a limo. You wanted me to wear a tux, I rented a tux. I paid for it all, Jen, because I wanted you to have a good time. The *least* you could do is enjoy yourself!

JENNY: How can I enjoy myself when you're dancing with other women? How can you say nothing was going on between the two of you? Do you think I'm blind? I was watching you the whole time. Everyone was watching. She was *hitting* on you. *(Mimicking.)* "Hold my hand, Joey. You look great in that tux, Joey. I hate that I don't have my own date tonight, Joey." God, it was sickening.

JOEY: Maybe she was flirting with me, Jen. But it didn't mean anything. Not to me anyway. She can flirt with me all she wants, it's not going to change how I feel about you.

JENNY: Really?

JOEY: I'm with you. Julia knows I'm with you.

JENNY: *(Softening.)* Then be with me, OK? Don't leave me by myself while you're out on the floor having the time of your life.

JOEY: Will you do me a favor?

JENNY: What?

JOEY: Stop being jealous of Julia.

JENNY: Do me a favor and stop dancing with her.

JOEY: Jen . . . take off your shoes.

JENNY: What? Why?

JOEY: Please . . . just take them off.

(She looks at him, a bit bewildered, but she takes off the shoes.)

JOEY: *(Extending his hand.)* Now . . . may I have this dance? Your shoes are off . . . you've got no excuse!

JENNY: *(Laughing, taking his hand.)* Sorry about my little meltdown. I just think we've got a good thing going and I don't want to lose you.

JOEY: You know something? You worry too much.

JENNY: I know.

JOEY: So quit worrying. Everything's great! And I'm gonna make you dance to every song, all night long, and you're gonna start having fun if it kills you!!

(They exit hand in hand moving off to the dance floor.)

END OF SCENE

REENTRY

LISA has recently returned to school after receiving treatment at an eating-disorder facility. She is nervous and hesitant as NIC attempts to make conversation.

NIC: Hey, Lisa! I haven't seen you in class for a long time. How are you?

LISA: *(Shyly.)* Fine. I'm fine.

NIC: How come you missed so much class?

LISA: I . . . um . . . I guess you could say I was . . . I was sick.

NIC: Oh? What was wrong?

LISA: I was sick.

NIC: I guess you don't want to talk about it.

LISA: Not really.

NIC: That's cool.

LISA: Well, I guess I'll see you around

NIC: Yeah. I'll see ya.

    (LISA starts to leave.)

NIC: *(Calling after her.)* Hey Lisa . . . wait! If you ever want to get together and play a game of tennis — that would be cool. I remember you used to be a good tennis player.

LISA: Oh. God, I haven't played in so long, Nic. I probably couldn't even hit the ball.

NIC: Well, maybe we could . . . I don't know. Maybe you'd want to do homework together some time?

LISA: I could use some help. I got way behind when I had to go to . . . when I was sick.

NIC: What was it? Like a burst appendix or something?

LISA: No.

NIC: Liver transplant?

LISA: *(Starts to laugh — then stops herself.)* Nic! That's not even funny.

NIC: I'm sorry. I guess I'm being too nosey. But some of the kids were talking and I heard certain things.

LISA: What did you hear?

NIC: Well . . . that you had a heart attack, which is so crazy. You're too young to have a heart attack.

LISA: Not that crazy.

NIC: What? Are you saying it's true?

LISA: Sort of. Look, Nic, if I tell you, will you please promise not to gossip about it. This isn't easy for me. Coming back to school and having everyone whispering and talking about me behind my back . . .

NIC: I promise Lis. I swear, I won't tell anyone.

LISA: You're sure?

NIC: Yeah. I totally promise.

LISA: *(Reluctantly.)* Well, I had an eating disorder. I wasn't eating. And I was exercising a lot. And taking these pills to help me lose weight and I didn't actually have a heart attack, but I could have. I got really weak and my heart was weak and I collapsed in gym one day when we were running laps. So they took me to the hospital and they said I needed to stay there for a while. Till I got stronger, ya know?

(NIC is silent.)

LISA: So, that's what happened.

NIC: *(A little stunned.)* But you're better now?

LISA: I'm working on it.

NIC: And you're eating again?

LISA: Slowly. But yeah, I'm eating. I feel stronger.

NIC: Well, that's good. I hope you stick around awhile.

LISA: Really?

NIC: Of course. I really like you, Lisa. I don't want you to be sick. And you shouldn't starve yourself. You'd look fine at any weight.

LISA: Wow! Thanks, Nic. That's one of the nicest things anyone has ever said to me.

NIC: Well, it's true. I'm just telling you the truth.

(There is a short pause — a little bit of an awkward silence.)

NIC: *(Breaking the silence.)* So, we'll do homework together? I'll help you catch up.

LISA: That would be so great. Thanks, Nic. Thank you for everything.

NIC: Hey, I didn't do anything special.

LISA: Believe me, you did. More than you know. I was so scared to come back to school — you're really the only person who has taken the time to talk to me.

NIC: But you have lots of friends.

LISA: They're all a little freaked out. They don't know *how* to talk to me.

NIC: Talking to you? There's nothing to it. So you want to come over today or what?

LISA: You can help me with the algebra?

NIC: *(Sighs heavily.)* Algebra? Well . . . I can try.

LISA: Let me call my mom, but I'm sure it'll be fine. I'll meet you here after last period, OK?

NIC: Great. And wait until you taste my mom's oatmeal chocolate-chip cookies. They're the best in the world. Eating them actually helps me with my algebra. Actually, I'm just jokin'. Nothing can help me with my algebra. But they're really good cookies!

LISA: Cookies?

NIC: *(Coaxing.)* Come on, Lis. A coupla cookies never hurt anyone.

LISA: Maybe just one. I'll try one.

NIC: Good! You're gonna be fine Lisa. I know you're gonna be just fine.

LISA: I hope so. I'm trying. And I really do appreciate all your help. I'll see you later, OK?

NIC: See ya. *(Watches her leave and then victoriously.)* YES!! Whoa — I better call Mom right away and tell her to bake some cookies . . . *fast!*

END OF SCENE

FRIENDLY RELATIONS

CARLA *is home from college for the Christmas holidays. Already bored with her family, she's anticipating having a miserable time during vacation. When her brother's friend JONATHAN arrives at the house, she feels he may help her to liven things up.*

CARLA: *(Running to the door after the doorbell rings three times and no one else has answered it.)* I'm coming . . . I'm coming. *(Shouting over her shoulder toward the back of the house.)* Geez, what do you guys do when I'm not here? Let the BUTLER answer the door? *(She opens the door and sees JONATHAN. She does not recognize him.)* Yes? Can I help you?

JONATHAN: Hi, Carla! Welcome home.

CARLA: Thanks. Are you selling candy or something?

JONATHAN: Carla! Don't your recognize me? I know we haven't seen each other for a while but I haven't changed *that* much, have I?

CARLA: I'm sorry . . . I don't . . . are you a friend of Brian's?

JONATHAN: Only his *best* friend.

CARLA: *(With slight recognition.)* Jimmy! How are you?

JONATHAN: Jonathan. My name's Jonathan. I'm fine. Thanks for remembering me.

CARLA: Jonathan. Of course. I'm sorry. I haven't been home for a while you know. I've been at school and last summer I was traveling. It's hard to keep up with all of Brian's little friends.

JONATHAN: I'm hardly *little* anymore.

CARLA: Where are my manners? Come in, come in. you're probably more at home here than I am.

JONATHAN: *(Coming in.)* Is Brian here?

CARLA: Actually, he ran to the store to get some stuff for my mom. But he'll be back any minute. Sit down. Do you want a coke or something?

JONATHAN: Sure, I'll have a coke. Did he take the car?

(CARLA goes out to the kitchen to get the drink. She speaks from offstage.)

CARLA: Yeah. My mom says it's such a pleasure that he has his license and she doesn't have to drive him everywhere. Do you drive?

JONATHAN: I'll get my license as soon as the holidays are over. My parents don't want me out on the road with all the drunks.

(CARLA enters with two drinks.)

CARLA: Makes sense. Here you go. Should we make a toast?

JONATHAN: Huh?

CARLA: You know, a toast. We'll drink a toast to . . . let's see? A Merry Christmas? Nah, too corny. A toast to you getting your license? How about a toast to getting to know each other better? *(She holds up her glass and encourages JONATHAN to do the same.)* Here's to getting to know you better, John. Down the hatch. *(She drinks it all in one gulp.)*

JONATHAN: *(Looking at her strangely.)* Jonathan. I go by Jonathan.

CARLA: Sorry. Well, drink up Jon-a-than.

JONATHAN: *(He sips the coke slowly.)* This tastes sorta funny. Is this decaffeinated?

CARLA: No, sweetie. It's actually got something extra special inside. Like a prize in your cereal box.

JONATHAN: What are you talking about?

CARLA: I put a little rum in your coke. For some holiday cheer.

JONATHAN: *(Startled. Immediately puts down his glass.)* Hey, I don't drink!

CARLA: What kind of a teenager are you? Don't you want to have some fun?

JONATHAN: I have plenty of fun thank you very much. I don't need to drink.

(CARLA leans closer into JONATHAN. She is very flirtatious.)

CARLA: Come on, John . . . Whoops, I mean Jonathan. We could have a lot of fun while I'm home. I'm sure Brian would be a good little brother and be willing to share you with me.

(JONATHAN stands abruptly. He is very flustered.)

JONATHAN: Look, Carla . . . you're a very nice person. And you're very pretty too. But . . . I just remembered something that I have to do. Just tell Brian I stopped by. I have to go.

(He starts for the door, but CARLA reaches him before he can escape.)

CARLA: Jonathan . . . don't be so uptight. We were just getting to know each other. Why don't you stay for dinner? On second thought, why don't you stay for the whole weekend?

(JONATHAN slowly backs away from CARLA in complete panic.)

JONATHAN: Hey . . . um . . . thanks for the invite, but I can't stay. I've gotta get home and help my mom. She wants me to . . . um . . . oh yeah, she told me I had to clean out the garage. She said that was going to be my big project for Christmas break. So . . . see . . . it's a big job . . . a really big job and I should probably get started on it right away . . . I should probably start on it right *now* . . . cause it's gonna take a long time to finish the whole thing. It'll probably take me the whole two weeks of vacation . . . I'm not gonna be able to do much of anything until I get that garage clean. Sparkling. My mom really likes things clean. So . . . um . . . sorry I can't stay . . . but . . . maybe some other time.

(CARLA is amused at his obvious panic. She stays standing directly in front of the door.)

CARLA: You sure are cute. I forgot how cute you were.

JONATHAN: Could you please . . . just . . . step away from the door?

CARLA: Step away from the door? What are you, a cop?

JONATHAN: I really need to leave.

CARLA: You're not gonna start to cry, are you?

JONATHAN: *(In frustration.)* Carla . . .

CARLA: *(Moving away from the door.)* OK, OK . . . I'm just having a little fun with you, that's all. Don't worry Jonathan — I won't hurt you. You can go now, if that's what you want.

JONATHAN: *(Slowly moves toward the door.)* Will you tell Brian I came by?

CARLA: Yes. And I'll tell him you'll be very busy cleaning out the garage so he shouldn't expect to see you until it's time to go back to school.

JONATHAN: Yeah, well . . . maybe it won't take me as long as I think it will. Well . . . bye. It was nice seeing you again . . . Carla. Merry Christmas.

(He quickly exits out the door.)

CARLA: Merry Christmas. *(Closes the door behind him.)* Damn, I gotta remember not to come on so strong . . . after all . . . he's only a high school kid. *(Lightheartedly.)* Oh, well — so much for *that* idea!

END OF SCENE

CONFESSIONS

AMY and PETER are socializing at an end-of-the-year barbeque at school. AMY discovers what a great guy PETER is and is quite drawn to him. She then confesses that her current boyfriend isn't nearly as wonderful as everyone seems to think he is.

AMY: I wish I hadn't waited till the end of the year to finally talk to you, Peter — I had no idea you were so funny. And so *nice*!

PETER: Well, that's me. I'm a nice, funny guy.

AMY: Are you gonna be around this summer?

PETER: Yeah . . . I have to go to summer school and if we *do* go anywhere after that's over, it'll only be for a couple of weeks.

AMY: Cool. Cause my birthday's in July and I'm probably gonna have a beach party. It'll be great if you could come.

PETER: That *would* be great.

AMY: I totally think you're cool. And *nice*.

PETER: Uh . . . thanks . . . you kinda already mentioned that.

AMY: Well, I guess I'm just not used to it.

PETER: What do you mean?

AMY: I'm just not used to guys being nice to me, that's all.

PETER: Really? Huh! I don't really know what to say about that. Why wouldn't guys be nice to you?

AMY: Well, it's not *all* guys. It's just one guy. My boyfriend.

PETER: Oh . . . you have a boyfriend?

AMY: Yeah, I guess I do.

PETER: Well, if you don't like him, or if he's mean to you — why don't you just break up with him?

AMY: It's a little complicated.

PETER: *(Uncertainly.)* Oh. Well . . . um . . . maybe things will start getting better between the two of you. Who is it? Do I know him?

AMY: Jake. Jake McLaren.

PETER: Jake McLaren the wrestler? The best wrestler on the school's team — *that* Jake McLaren?

AMY: That's the guy.

PETER: Wow! I wouldn't want to break up with him either.

AMY: What's that supposed to mean?

PETER: *(Awkwardly.)* Well . . . he's awesome! I mean . . . uh . . . uh . . . what I'm trying to say is . . . I don't like him like *that* . . . of course not . . . I'm just saying he's such a great athlete and he seems really cool and . . . I . . . I . . .

AMY: *(Slightly amused as she watches him flounder.)* I know what you mean. He's great-looking. He's a popular jock. Why wouldn't I want to be with his girlfriend, right?

PETER: Yeah. Exactly.

AMY: *(Ironically.)* All the girls are jealous of me because I've got such a big stud for a boyfriend.

PETER: Well you don't sound very happy about it.

AMY: Like I said, it's complicated.

PETER: Do you want to tell me why?

AMY: I don't know if I should. But God, Peter, you're so easy to talk to and it would be nice to vent about things my girl-friends just don't seem to understand. Do you mind?

PETER: Are you kidding? Vent away.

AMY: Well just because Jake is good-looking and popular and a star athlete, everyone naturally assumes that he's this great guy.

PETER: And he's not?

AMY: Well . . . he's not very . . . polite.

PETER: You mean he's rude?

AMY: Well, he's gotten people to do things for him his whole life. His family adores him, his teachers adore him, and all the kids at school treat him as if he were some famous rock star or something. I can't blame them . . . I did it too; be-fore I really knew what he was like. But lately — he thinks I'm his personal slave. He treats me like I'm his errand girl or something. And . . . well . . . this is very personal, so please don't say anything . . .

PETER: I would never, I promise.

AMY: Well . . . it's gotten to the point where he's starting to pressure me into doing things I don't want to do. If you know what I mean?

PETER: Oh . . . I think I do.

AMY: He's really been hassling me lately about . . . ya know . . . *that!* I don't want to and the more he pressures me, the less I want to. See — I told you it was complicated.

PETER: So break up with him. You don't need anyone treating you like that! Why don't you do it?

AMY: Well it's just that ever since we started going out, I've had more friends than I've ever had in my life. It totally elevated my status, ya know? It's a dumb reason to stay with someone, but that part of it has been great. I just know that if we break up everyone will naturally assume he broke up with me and I'll go back to being plain-old-nothing Amy.

PETER: You could never be plain-old-nothing Amy. And did you ever think that the people who drop you because you're no longer Jake's girlfriend aren't your real friends anyway?

AMY: Yeah. I know. They just hang around me to get to him — I know that. I'm aware of that. But I like it anyway. I don't really think I have any "real" friends.

PETER: *(Kindly.)* You do now.

AMY: See — that's what I mean — you're *so* nice. About everything.

PETER: I mean it. I'm your friend. And I don't understand how Jake could treat a girl like that. Especially you.

AMY: Thanks, Peter. Maybe I will break up with him. If I do, then I could date other people. Nicer people.

PETER: Uh . . . yeah, exactly.

AMY: Maybe I could even date you?

PETER: Me? You'd want to go out with *me?*

AMY: I thought I was making that very clear during this entire conservation. Yes! I'd totally go out with you. You're the nicest guy I've ever met. And right now, I could use that in my life.

PETER: Awesome. That's totally awesome. Well . . . now I definitely think you should break up with Jake. Cause this could actually be the greatest summer of my life!

(AMY looks at him questioningly.)

PETER: No pressure, of course!

AMY: *(Laughing.)* Of course! Well, Pete, can I call you Pete? Let's just wait and see what might happen.

PETER: Yeah . . . let's just wait and see . . .

END OF SCENE

SISTERLY ADVICE

*As KATIE is busy in the kitchen making herself some-
thing to eat, her younger brother TOBY seeks her out
to ask her for some advice regarding his physique.*

TOBY: Hey! Uh . . . what are you doing?

KATIE: *(Preparing a sandwich.)* What does it look like I'm
doing, dorkus?

TOBY: I don't know . . . making a sandwich?

KATIE: *(Quite sarcastically.)* Oh, my God! Alert the media . .
. my brother is a genius!

TOBY: *(Obviously a little uncomfortable.)* Ha, ha . . . that was
a good one! Sis!

KATIE: What do you want, dorkus? If it's a sandwich — make
your own, I'm not your maid.

TOBY: No . . . I don't want one. I mean it looks good . . . it
looks *great* — but I don't want anything.

KATIE: Good! So take a hike, would you, so I can eat this without having to stare at your ugly face. Wouldn't want to lose
my appetite, ya know.

TOBY: *(Earnestly.)* Could you quit it for a second?

KATIE: Quit what?

TOBY: The put-downs for one second. I need to ask you
somethin'.

KATIE: You said you didn't want anything!

TOBY: Well, I do. I just don't know how to ask you. Without
you laughing at me.

KATIE: Money? You want money? Cause if you want money,
I'm not laughing!

TOBY: No. It's not that. Besides, you don't have any money
anyway.

KATIE: Sad, but true. So what then?

TOBY: Advice.

KATIE: *You* want advice from *me*! That is the best joke I've heard all week.

TOBY: It's no joke. I'm not kidding, Kate. I really could use your help.

KATIE: *(Realizing he's serious.)* What's going on?

TOBY: It's embarrassing.

KATIE: Ohhhhhh . . . well maybe you shouldn't be talking to me about this. Maybe you should talk to Mom . . . or better yet . . . talk to Dad if it's a — ya know — "man" thing.

TOBY: No, no — nothing like that! I need to talk to you. 'Cause . . . it's just that . . . lately, I've noticed that . . .

KATIE: Oh c'mon — you're killing me! Just tell me already, would you?

TOBY: *(Blurting it out quickly.)* I've got love handles.

KATIE: You've got what?

TOBY: Love handles . . . in the back . . . on my back.

KATIE: What are you talking about? You're too young for love handles.

TOBY: Well, I have 'em. *(Lifts up shirt and turns around.)* See?

KATIE: Wow! I guess you do. Better hit the gym, little brother.

TOBY: Well, that's what I want to talk to you about.

KATIE: *(Suspiciously.)* What?

TOBY: Can you help me get rid of them?

KATIE: What do you want me to do — get the vacuum cleaner and give you liposuction?

TOBY: C'mon, Katie, I'm serious. You're always on a diet. You could tell me what to eat. I gotta get rid of 'em.

KATIE: *(Softening when she sees how desperate he is.)* Tobes, it's baby fat. You're gonna grow pretty soon. A growth spurt, they call it. It's bound to happen in the next year or so. It'll take care of itself. You *don't* need to go on a diet!

TOBY: But I look like a middle-aged man!

KATIE: No, you don't! Why are so worried about this all of a sudden?

(TOBY shrugs.)

KATIE: Why?

TOBY: *(Muttering under his breath.)* Pool party at Jeff's house next Saturday.

KATIE: So?

TOBY: So? So . . . I don't want Melissa Kramer to see me without a shirt, OK?

KATIE: *(Teasing him again.)* Awwww . . . little Toby's got a crush!

TOBY: Cut it out! Will you help me or not?

KATIE: I told you, you don't need a diet! And even if I did help you — even if I put you on some strict diet of nothing but lettuce and apples and made you run ten miles every day, those things still wouldn't be gone by next Saturday.

TOBY: *(Slightly defeated.)* Yeah, I guess you're right. Maybe I just won't go.

KATIE: Oh give me a break! Don't be such a little girl. My God — she's not even gonna notice!

TOBY: Really? You think?

KATIE: Melissa Kramer, huh? Which one is she?

TOBY: Red curly hair — taller than me. Really, really pretty.

KATIE: Well, that figures.

TOBY: So I shouldn't even bother, huh?

KATIE: No. Don't stress over it. I'm telling you, in six months or a year, we're gonna be calling you stretch! And bye, bye love handles, hello Melissa Kramer!

TOBY: *(Reluctantly.)* OK. I hope you're right. I hope it happens by next week though.

(KATIE goes back to eating her sandwich.)

TOBY: *(Sweetly.)* So . . . since I'm *not* going on a diet . . . ya know, your sandwich looks *really* good . . . will you make me one too?

KATIE: Fat chance! Make your own — and go easy on the mayo, chubby!

TOBY: Hey!

END OF SCENE

QUID PRO QUO

NANCY, *a very pretty and popular student, is failing her science class and asks PHILIP, the class genius, to help her out by becoming her lab partner. PHILIP agrees to do it, only if he can get something in return from NANCY.*

NANCY: Philip! Hey, Philip — wait up — I need to ask you something.

PHILIP: *(Looking around, confused.)* You mean me?

NANCY: Your name *is* Philip, isn't it?

PHILIP: Well . . . yeah . . . but . . . I didn't think you even knew who I was.

NANCY: I know you. Of course I know you. You're in my science class. That's what I want to talk to you about.

PHILIP: You want to talk to me?

NANCY: Yeah — do you have a lab partner?

PHILIP: Are you kidding?

NANCY: No — I'm not kidding. Do you have one?

PHILIP: Nope.

PHILIP: So, could I be your partner? I need one.

PHILIP: *You* need a lab partner? I figured *you* of all people would have about a hundred people wanting to be partners with you.

NANCY: Don't you think you're exaggerating just a little bit?

PHILIP: Well — you always seem to have tons of people around you at any given time. I just figured you wouldn't have any trouble finding a lab partner. And why would you want me anyway?

NANCY: I want someone who can help me get a good grade. You're practically a genius, Philip. Everyone knows that. I could really use your help. I may be flunking this class — and that *cannot* happen. So, will you?

PHILIP: There's gotta be a catch.

NANCY: There's no catch. I need a partner — you need a partner — I'll work really hard, I'm not asking you to carry me, but I don't get a lot of the stuff and I . . . I guess I *need* you. What do you say?

PHILIP: Well, Haskins asked me to partner with him about ten minutes ago.

NANCY: Oh. Haskins?

PHILIP: Yeah. Jimmy. James Haskins. Jimmy. I was gonna — but now — uh — I could tell him I found someone else.

NANCY: Would you? That would be awesome. I'd really appreciate it. I'd owe you big.

PHILIP: You'd owe me?

NANCY: Well, if you help me pass this class — yeah! I'd owe you big time!

PHILIP: Like what? Like what would you do?

NANCY: I don't know — buy you a CD or something. *(Suspiciously.)* Why? What would you want?

PHILIP: Go out with me. That's what I'd want.

NANCY: Do what?

PHILIP: Go out with me.

NANCY: Out where?

PHILIP: On a date. Go with me on a date.

NANCY: A date? Uh . . . I don't know about that.

PHILIP: Why not? You said you'd owe me. You asked me what I wanted? I help you. You help me. It's called quid pro quo.

NANCY: Quid pro quo. Yeah, I've heard that before. That was in *Silence of the Lambs* right?

PHILIP: Yeah. Right. So . . . will you do it?

NANCY: If I say I can't do it — then no lab partner?

PHILIP: That's right.

NANCY: Can't I just buy you something?

PHILIP: Am I that repulsive to you, Nancy? Is that it? You can't possibly imagine being seen with me in public?

NANCY: No! No! Of course not. That's not it at all. It's just . . .

PHILIP: Yes? Just what?

NANCY: I don't know.

PHILIP: Look — you need the grade. I need a date. I'm not asking a lot. One date.

NANCY: Just one?

PHILIP: Yeah — I'm not asking to be your boyfriend or anything. *Please!* I'm a reasonable man!

NANCY: When?

PHILIP: Saturday night.

NANCY: Oh, I can't this Saturday night. I've got . . . I've got plans. It'll have to be some other time.

PHILIP: OK. What's good for you?

NANCY: Monday. We can go next Monday.

PHILIP: A Monday, huh? Not exactly a date night.

NANCY: Well, my weekends are pretty booked, so . . . Monday, possibly Tuesday . . . that's the best I can do.

PHILIP: OK. Monday it is.

NANCY: So . . . we go out just once. On Monday. And then you'll be my lab partner for the rest of the semester?

PHILIP: Yeah. Pretty good deal, right?

NANCY: Sure. It's great. OK. Well . . . thanks, I guess. And I guess we can talk about Monday later in the week.

PHILIP: Ya know, Nancy . . . a miracle might happen . . .

NANCY: You mean, I might actually pass Chemistry?

PHILIP: I was thinking that the miracle might be that you actually have a good time Monday night.

NANCY: *(Hurriedly.)* Oh. Yeah. I'm sure it'll be fine. So I'll see ya . . . . *(She runs off.)*

PHILIP: Yeah. See ya. *(Watching her leave.)* A date with Nancy Browning! Ha! I *am* a genius!

END OF SCENE

MISUNDERSTANDING

MATT and CLAIRE are best friends, though CLAIRE'S feelings run deeper. MATT, however, is gay, although CLAIRE does not realize this. She thinks he's trying to tell her that he has stronger feelings for her, when in fact he is telling her about the feelings he has for another guy.

MATT: Are you ready for this big news of mine?

CLAIRE: Yeah. Totally. You sounded like you were going to burst over the phone. What's so major?

MATT: Well . . . there's this person that I have been having feelings for — for a while now, ya know, but I didn't think they felt the same way. But now, I'm pretty sure they do.

CLAIRE: Really? Who?

MATT: Well I know you're my best friend and everything — but I'm not quite ready to tell you who it is yet.

CLAIRE: Oh. OK. Um . . . well . . . how do you know that they feel the same way about you?

MATT: Well, lately we've been spending so much time together. And we like the same stuff, ya know? Same music. Same movies. And it's just a feeling I get because they haven't said anything to me . . . but it's the way we look at each other, ya know?

CLAIRE: Yeah. I do. I know very well. So what do you think? Are you gonna say something?

MATT: I'm dying to. I really want to tell them how I feel. But what if the worst thing in the world happens.

CLAIRE: What do you mean? The worst thing in the world?

MATT: Well, if I blurt out my feelings and tell them how I feel about them — that I've felt this way for a long time — the worst thing would be if they didn't feel the same way. Then I look like a total moron.

CLAIRE: But don't you think that you should trust your instincts?

MATT: I want to. I want to trust them.

CLAIRE: And what do your instincts tell you?

MATT: That this person feels the same way about me. I guess maybe we're both too shy to say anything. And if no one ever says anything *then* where will I be?

CLAIRE: Right! So I think you should make your move. Ask this person out on a date. A real date. Not just two friends hanging out.

MATT: Oh, my God. Just thinking about doing that makes me have a stomachache. But it's also something that I really want to do.

CLAIRE: Then I think you should go for it.

MATT: Really? Oh, Claire — you're the best! *(He pulls her to him and hugs her.)* What would I do without you?

CLAIRE: I seriously don't know. So, you're gonna do it?

MATT: Yeah! Today. Right now.

CLAIRE: Right now?

MATT: Yeah! Might as well do it now. Trust my instincts like you said. Hopefully, it'll all be good, ya know? They'll want to be with me too.

CLAIRE: Who wouldn't want to be with you?

MATT: Sweet! You're such a sweetie! OK, so I wasn't going to do this, but you've been so incredibly supportive you deserve to know who this person is that I've been talking about.

CLAIRE: *(Hesitantly.)* Well, I kind of think I know.

MATT: You do?

CLAIRE: I think I might.

MATT: Well, who do you think it is? Tell me and I'll tell you if you're right or not.

CLAIRE: I'm a little embarrassed.

MATT: I know, I know! Me too! That's why I couldn't bring myself to tell you before. So . . . do you really think you know?

(Their next lines are spoken in unison.)

CLAIRE: It's me.   MATT: It's Mike.

(There's a pause as they look at each other a bit stunned.)

CLAIRE: Wait a minute — what did you say?

MATT: What did you say?

CLAIRE: *(Slowly, carefully.)* I said "it's me." The way you were describing this *person* . . . it sounded like me. It sounded like all the things you and I do together. And I thought you knew how I felt about you. And that I've felt this way for a long time.

MATT: Oh, my God. The worst thing happened — it's just opposite of what I thought.

CLAIRE: Matt! Did you say Mike? You want to be with *Mike?!*

MATT: Yeah . . . I'm afraid so. I thought you knew.

CLAIRE: How could I know?

MATT: I thought you knew I was gay.

CLAIRE: I didn't know. Maybe I didn't want to know. God — I'm such an idiot.

MATT: No — it's totally my fault. We should have talked about this a long time ago. I should have said something. I think I sort of knew you liked me that way — and I liked it. It made me feel good to know you had a little crush on me. But, that's what I thought it was — a little crush — because I thought you knew.

CLAIRE: I've gotta go.

MATT: Claire *please* don't go. Let's talk about this.

CLAIRE: No. I don't want to. I . . . I don't feel very good . . . and you have to go find Mike.

MATT: I'm not gonna do that now. Claire — you're my best friend. Let's talk about this.

CLAIRE: No. Not now. I've gotta go.

(MATT tries to approach her and hug her again; she shrugs him off and exits.)

END OF SCENE

SPLIT

CHRIS breaks the news to his younger sister JILL that their parents have decided to get a divorce.

CHRIS: Jill? Jilly? Can I talk to you for a minute?

JILL: How many times have I told you, don't call me Jilly?

CHRIS: OK. Sorry. But we need to talk.

JILL: Oh? Why? What's going on?

CHRIS: I need to tell you somethin'.

JILL: God, you sound so serious. Did somebody die?

CHRIS: Not exactly.

JILL: Not exactly? What's that supposed to mean?

CHRIS: No one died.

JILL: Good. So what's the big deal?

CHRIS: It's Mom and Dad.

JILL: What about them?
 (CHRIS hesitates — not exactly sure how to tell her the news.)

JILL: Chris — tell *me!* What about Mom and Dad? Are they sick?

CHRIS: No. No one is sick.

JILL: Then what? The suspense is killing me.

CHRIS: Well — it looks like they're gonna split up.

JILL: Split up? Mom and Dad?

CHRIS: They wanted me to tell you first.

JILL: *(Shocked.)* They're getting a divorce?

CHRIS: Looks that way, I'm afraid.

JILL: They can't do this. They can't do this to *us!*

CHRIS: It's not really about us, Jill. They can't stand each other. Haven't you noticed?

JILL: But . . . but . . . it's not that bad. I see them laughing together sometimes.

CHRIS: When? When was the last time you saw them laugh at

something the other one said. They act like strangers, Jill. They've only been staying together because of us.

JILL: Well they *should* stay together because of us — that's exactly what I'm saying!

CHRIS: There is so much tension in this house sometimes it makes me want to scream. Are you that self-absorbed?

JILL: Shut up! I'm not self-absorbed! I just thought they were having some minor problems. That's normal.

CHRIS: Jill, wake up! I know you know what I'm talking about. I know you turn up your stereo or put your earphones on to avoid hearing their screaming matches. It's gonna be a lot better after Dad leaves.

JILL: When is he leaving? And how do you know all this and I'm just hearing it all for the first time?

CHRIS: Mom told me — and she's really upset and she thought it would be better if you heard all of this from me. Dad rented an apartment and he'll be gone by the weekend.

JILL: Why can't they get therapy like other couples?

CHRIS: You don't even know what you're talking about. They've done it all. They've tried to work things out — it's over.

JILL: So that's it? We have no say in this? Our lives are completely turned upside down and there's nothing we can do about it?

CHRIS: It's their marriage.

JILL: But we're *their* kids! This affects us! Now we're gonna come from a broken home just like everybody else we know.

CHRIS: I know. It's weird. Out of all my friends, I was like the only one who lived with both parents. But still . . . there's nothing we can do.

JILL: Now we have to live in two places and spend time separately with Mom and Dad, so there goes all my free time. I know how it works and it sucks. And one of them is bound to get remarried. There'll be other kids to deal with and a stepmom or stepdad. I can't believe this is happening to me.

CHRIS: It's happening to me too! And what about them? You

think they're happy about this? You think their lives aren't totally disrupted? God, I can't believe that all you can think about is how this inconveniences you. You're such a spoiled little girl, Jill.

JILL: Why are you being so mean to me? I thought you were supposed to be the one to help me get through this. Isn't that why Mom asked you to tell me?

CHRIS: I'm not trying to be mean. I knew you'd be upset, but I thought you would be concerned for all of us — not just how this affects *your* life. It's gonna be hard for everybody — we have to support each other. You have no idea what this is doing to Mom. Try to put yourself in her shoes and be a little more considerate of her feelings. The last thing she needs is to hear you complain that you now have to live in two places. We all have to make adjustments, Jill. Try to be more caring.

JILL: You come in here and drop this major bomb on me, and then you give me a lecture that I'm not a good person. It's all too much to handle right now, Chris.

CHRIS: I'm sorry. But things around here are changing. And the sooner you realize that, the better off you'll be. Like I said before, Jill, it's time for you to grow up — maybe it's happening sooner than you'd like — but you better face the fact that life can't always be what you want it to be.

JILL: What? Dad's moving out, so you're now taking his place by lecturing me about how harsh life is?

CHRIS: I'm not trying to be Dad — I'm just trying to let you know that things around here are going to be very different.

JILL: I realize that, Chris. Why do you think I'm so upset?

CHRIS: Different doesn't necessarily mean bad. Maybe it'll be the best thing that ever happened to us. Maybe it'll make us appreciate each other more and not take things for granted.

JILL: Doubtful.

CHRIS: Well — they're taking us out to dinner at seven tonight to talk about it. A family meeting. I guess we're going out to a restaurant so they can't start screaming at each other. Try not to be a butt hole about it, OK?

JILL: You're the butt hole!

CHRIS: Oh, that's mature.

JILL: I was trying to make a joke. God, can't you even take a joke?

CHRIS: Be ready to go by seven, OK?

JILL: Our lives are ruined.

CHRIS: Not ruined! Just changed. And change can be good.

JILL: Whatever.

CHRIS: Hate to break it to ya, Sis, but you're gonna have to grow up whether you like it or not. Get used to it.

(CHRIS exits. JILL is left alone still feeling shocked by the news.)

JILL: I'll never get used to *this*.

END OF SCENE

LOST IN THE WOODS

ERIN and DANNY are in the car on their way to visit their friend Scott whose family has a cabin in the mountains. ERIN becomes panicked when it seems DANNY is lost and she allows her imagination to go into overdrive.

ERIN: This is great! Just great! You have no idea where we are, do you?

DANNY: I kinda know. I'm pretty sure that if we follow this road, it'll curve around and take us to the turnoff, which leads to the cabin.

ERIN: Pretty sure?

DANNY: Almost sure?

ERIN: Danny, we've been driving for hours. Why can't you just admit that we're lost?

DANNY: I don't think we are. I've been up to Scott's cabin before. This all looks pretty familiar.

ERIN: How can it look familiar? It's all trees! Just miles and miles of trees . . . and it's starting to get dark — we're never gonna find this place in the dark! Just stop the car and ask for directions, would you?

DANNY: You just said it's all trees, so where am I supposed to stop? And *who* should I ask for directions? The axe murderer that lives in the woods?

ERIN: That's not even funny.

DANNY: It is kinda creepy up here, huh? *(In a spooky voice.)* Who knows what evil lurks beyond the forest walls . . . *(He lets out a loud evil laugh.)*

ERIN: Knock it off!! Stop trying to scare me. Just call him, OK? Call Scott — you *did* bring the cell phone, didn't you?

DANNY: Yeah. It's back there — get it for me, will you?

(ERIN reaches into the backseat and pulls DANNY'S cell

phone out of his bag. She turns on the cell phone and starts to dial, but gets no service.)

ERIN: Oh, that figures! No service! There's no service up here! Now what are we gonna do?

DANNY: I gotta pee.

ERIN: Where is this place anyway? There's nothing out here. I haven't seen one single house since we left that main road about an hour ago.

DANNY: That's why it's called the woods, Erin. Nothing out here but . . . *woods!*

ERIN: Yeah, but when Scott said his parents had a cabin in the woods, I thought he meant some quaint little mountain town — ya know, with a general store and a gas station that had a phone that actually worked or a guy you could ask directions and maybe they would have a bathroom! A bathroom would be nice.

DANNY: Geez, calm down, would ya? God, you're freakin' out on me. I'll find the place, don't worry. But first, I really gotta pee.

(DANNY pulls over to the side of the road and brings the car to a stop.)

ERIN: What's going on? What are you doing?

DANNY: I'm gonna go relieve myself. Out in the woods — on a tree — like a real man!

ERIN: You're gonna leave me here by myself?

DANNY: Unless you want to come with me . . . but to tell you the truth, I'd like a little privacy. Well — as much privacy as you can have out here.

ERIN: *(Panicked.)* Don't leave me here. What about that axe murderer you were talking about?

DANNY: I was *kidding.* Ya know, I think you've seen *Scream* one too many times! Relax. I'll be a second.

ERIN: Well hurry up, OK? I really need to go too, but I'm not peeing in the woods. I'll wait. Hurry up!

DANNY: You're such a city girl. OK — I'll be right back.

(DANNY walks off.)

ERIN: *(Calling out to him.)* Stay where I can see you!

DANNY: *(Offstage.)* No way!

ERIN: Well, don't go too far. Whistle or something.

DANNY: *(Offstage.)* Geez, you are truly para —

(DANNY cuts off abruptly. ERIN is now in a full-blown panic.)

ERIN: Danny? Danny? Quit goofing around. Danny? Answer me! This is *so* not funny. Danny? I swear to God, if you're not already dead I'm gonna kill you! DANNY!! *Please!* Answer me! *(She checks the car to see if the keys are in the ignition.)* Oh, my God! I can't even go for help — he took the keys! DANNY!! Oh God, why is this happening? It *is* just like in the movies. OK. I've got to calm down. I need to remain calm. What would that girl in *Scream* do?

(DANNY comes up behind ERIN very matter-of-factly as if nothing were wrong.)

DANNY: Hey, I think I found the cabin!

(ERIN screams and spins around to see DANNY grinning at her with his good news.)

ERIN: Oh, my God! Where did you come from? Didn't you hear me screaming for you? I thought you were being murdered. I thought your bloody corpse was about to be thrown across the hood of this car! Why didn't you answer me? I nearly peed in my pants when you came sneaking up behind me, you jerk!

DANNY: Erin, come on, chill! I said I think I found the cabin. Isn't that great? It's just on the other side of these trees. I told you it looked familiar. I guess I must have missed the turnoff before. I know how to get there now.

ERIN: Thank God. Man, I was about to have a heart attack. Don't ever do that to me again, OK?

DANNY: You crack me up. You're all worked up over nothing. You scared yourself! Now come on — let's go. Scott's gonna wonder what happened to us.

(They get back into the car.)

ERIN: I can't wait to finally use the bathroom. First thing I'm
   gonna do!
DANNY: Oh Erin — didn't I tell you? Scott's family really likes
   to rough it up here. No electricity. No running water. But
   hey — cheer up! You don't have to go in the woods. They
   do have an outhouse!
(At this new information, ERIN looks on the verge of tears.)
ERIN: Can we just turn around and go home now? I *hate* the
   woods!

END OF SCENE

STALKED

At the shopping mall, SHANNON finally confronts JOEL, the guy she feels has been following her obsessively for the past few weeks.

SHANNON: *(Turning around abruptly to face JOEL.)* LOOK! I know you're following me; I know you've *been* following me like every single day for the last week or so . . . just get lost already, you big wacko!

JOEL: *(Innocently.)* Hey . . . I don't know what you're talking about. I have just as much right to be here as you do.

SHANNON: You're *always* where I happen to be. How do you explain that?

JOEL: Coincidence?

SHANNON: Yeah, right. Since when do guys shop at The Limited?

JOEL: I have to get a gift for my sister.

SHANNON: Just stay away from me! Pervert!
(She starts to walk away.)

JOEL: I don't know why you're so upset; I haven't done *anything* to you . . . *(Muttering under his breath.)* Yet.

SHANNON: *(Whirling back around to face him.)* What did you say?

JOEL: *(In a singsong voice.)* I said have a nice day!

SHANNON: If you have something to say to me, say it! Don't be some creepy little coward who doesn't have the guts to speak his mind.

JOEL: Hey! I'm not a coward — take that back.

SHANNON: *(Laughing at him.)* What are you, ten? *(Mimicking him.)* "Take that back, take that back!"

JOEL: *(Angrily.)* You just think you're so smart, don't you, Shannon. It must be nice always being little Miss Perfect.

SHANNON: How do you know my name?

JOEL: I know everything about you.

SHANNON: OK . . . that's it . . . I'm reporting you to the police, you weirdo. *(She starts walking away to find security.)* Right now!

JOEL: *(Calling after her.)* Wait! Wait! You know me too. You *used* to know me.

SHANNON: *(She stops and faces him again.)* What are you talking about?

JOEL: We went to elementary school together. Don't you remember? We were at different middle schools, but now we're in the same school again, isn't that great? Except I've tried saying hi to you, like a million times, and you always ignore me. That's kind of rude, Shannon.

SHANNON: So you decide to *stalk* me? And make *threats*?

JOEL: I never threatened you.

SHANNON: You just did — awhile ago. "I haven't done anything to you — *yet!*" That sounds like a threat to me. You're sick!

JOEL: I'm just trying to get your attention.

SHANNON: Well now you have it. And I think you're going to have the attention of the police pretty soon if you don't stop following me.

JOEL: Do you remember me? Joel. I'm Joel Sykes from Lake Drive Elementary. Remember?

SHANNON: No. I've never seen you before in my life. Except for the past couple of weeks. You're there every time I turn around. You're a freak.

JOEL: *(Calmly as if he doesn't have a care in the world.)* I guess I look a lot different. The last time you saw me I was like . . . ya know . . . eleven or something. I've grown a lot since then.

SHANNON: The last time I saw you, you were spying on me and my friends at Starbucks.

JOEL: You look exactly the same only taller. You were always the prettiest girl in school.

SHANNON: OK . . . that's *it!* I'm finding a cop.

JOEL: What did I say? I'm trying to give you a compliment, and you act as if I've assaulted you.

SHANNON: Don't you get it? You give me the creeps! How much clearer can I be? You know all this stuff about me and I know nothing about you; I don't remember *ever* knowing you — in elementary school or any other time for that matter. I swear to God, *Joel*, or whatever your name is — if I see you lurking by my house or anywhere else, I'm reporting you. Here's my message loud and clear: *Leave me alone!*

JOEL: They can't do anything to me if I haven't done anything to you.

SHANNON: You wanna bet? This state has stalking laws. I did a speech on it — I know all about it. I *can* get a restraining order. And I will if I have to.

JOEL: You're flattering yourself *Shannon!* Why would I stalk *you* — you're not exactly some famous celebrity or anything.

SHANNON: For your information, people other than celebrities get stalked too. It happens all the time. And I don't know why you're following me . . . but it better stop! I'm not kidding. I can dish out threats too, pig!

JOEL: *(Slightly shaken by her aggressiveness.)* Well . . . I'm *not* stalking you!

SHANNON: Good! So you don't have anything to worry about. And I'll never see you again after today. If I do, I'm warning you — you'll be in big trouble. Stay away from me, *Joe.* *(She turns from him and walks away.)*

JOEL: *(Calling after her.)* It's JOEL! And I can't help it if we run into each other at school.

SHANNON: *(Without turning around she yells back.)* Stay away! *(SHANNON exits.)*

JOEL: *(Looking after SHANNON he talks to himself.)* I can't help it if I just *happen* to transfer into your English class. Ya gotta take English if you want to get into a good college. Won't be my fault if we happen to wind up in the same class . . . won't be my fault at all . . .

END OF SCENE

THE NICKNAME

*After NIKKI proves her athletic status, her brother
GAVIN decides to give her a nickname. NIKKI, however, is quite insulted with what he has come up with.*

GAVIN: Hey you! Mom said you came in first in that 10K race
you ran.

NIKKI: Yeah, isn't that cool? All that training paid off, I guess.

GAVIN: Way to go, Beef!

NIKKI: What did you call me?

GAVIN: Beef! It's a cool nickname, don'tcha think? Every athlete needs a nickname. You can be Beef.

NIKKI: What kind of a nickname is Beef?

GAVIN: Solid. Sturdy. Substantial. BEEF!

NIKKI: No! Absolutely not! I reject it! Where in the world did
you come up with that?

GAVIN: Well, c'mon, Nik. Your legs have always been a bit . . .
ya know.

NIKKI: A bit what?

GAVIN: A bit . . . big. On the beefy side, ya know?

NIKKI: Shut up! I can't believe you just said that. I absolutely
hate you right now.

GAVIN: Well it's a good thing to have big legs. You're a runner . . . you're strong. Your legs are strong. I mean, you came
in first, right, kiddo? That's awesome!

NIKKI: There — you just called me kiddo. Let "kiddo" be my
nickname.

GAVIN: Nah — that's no good. Can't you see it? We're all at
the Olympics. You're ready to run the race against some of
the fastest people in the world. The gun goes off and you
hear the crowd start to chant, "Beef, Beef, Beef, Beef!"

NIKKI: *(Sarcastically.)* Oh yeah! That would really be motivating.

GAVIN: It would be amazing. I'm gonna spread the word. I'll

e-mail everyone. Start calling Nikki "Beef." We'll all come to your next track meet and chant.

NIKKI: Don't you dare! If you do, I swear to God, I will kill you! I don't want to be known as Beef. It's defintely the worst nickname I've ever heard. It's insulting!

GAVIN: You're missing the point. It's not insulting at all. People will remember you. *And* respect you!

NIKKI: I do *not* want to be remembered for having big legs! You're such a moron. If I'm a fast runner, call me Flash or Kid Speed — something like that. Not Beef! You have absolutely no sensitivity at all.

GAVIN: Hey, I'm just trying to help you make a name for yourself. Pardon me for trying to be clever.

NIKKI: I don't think it's clever.

GAVIN: I can see that.

NIKKI: Come up with something else. If you come up with something better, *maybe* I'll use it.

GAVIN: Ohhhh . . . so you *do* want a nickname.

NIKKI: Yeah . . . it's actually a good idea. I like the part when you chant my name at the Olympics. But come up with something better than part of a cow.

GAVIN: OK. I'll work on it. Although I'll always be partial to Beef.

NIKKI: Don't even think about it.

GAVIN: *(Giving this serious thought.)* Flash . . . Kid Speed . . . they're not original enough.

NIKKI: So? You said you were clever. Come up with something original. That's your new mission in life.

GAVIN: *(Suddenly gets an idea.)* I've got it — it just came to me this second. Oh, you're gonna love this one.

NIKKI: What is it?

GAVIN: *(Proudly.)* Butterball. It's easy to chant. Rolls off the tongue. Butterball! Butterball! Butterball! Yup! That's it.

NIKKI: Are you out of your mind? First I'm a cow and now I'm a turkey? You're nuts!

GAVIN: *(Hopefully.)* Should we go back to using Beef then?

NIKKI: No! Forget it. Forget the whole nickname thing. Forget the chanting. I don't even want to go to the Olympics.

GAVIN Gosh, Nik. I didn't mean for you to throw away your entire running career over a stupid little name. I think it's great that you're a track star. Keep it up, OK?

NIKKI I really like doing this, ya know? Especially the winning part. But stop with the nicknames, OK? Just forget the idea. You can chant Nikki if you want to, but nothing else, OK?

GAVIN: *(Reluctantly.)* All right. But can I call you Beef when we're at home? When no one else is around?

NIKKI: Only if I can call you Warped Brain.

GAVIN: Uh . . . OK! Deal!

(They shake hands.)

END OF SCENE

BLACKMAIL

ERICA comes home very late to find her younger brother MARCUS sitting up waiting for her. MARCUS tries to manipulate ERICA into telling him where she's been all night, but she finds a way to turn the tables on him.

ERICA is seen quietly sneaking into a dark house. MARCUS is waiting for her, sitting in the dark. As she enters, he snaps on the light and startles her.

MARCUS: It's mighty late, little girl.

ERICA: Oh God! You scared me to death! You sounded just like Dad.

MARCUS: Where were you?

ERICA: Out.

MARCUS: With?

ERICA: None of your business.

MARCUS: Do you know what time it is?

ERICA: No.

MARCUS: It's two-thirty.

ERICA: So what are you doing up so late?

MARCUS: I couldn't sleep — went to snag some CDs out of your room and saw you weren't there. You're so lucky Mom and Dad aren't up. You would be so dead!

ERICA: But you're gonna keep that trap of yours shut like a good little brother so they'll never know, right? And by the way, don't go into my room again! Ever! Unless you're invited, which isn't likely to happen anytime soon.

MARCUS: Where were you?

ERICA: I told you — *out!* Now drop it!

MARCUS: With who? How come you're so late?

ERICA: Mucus . . . I'm serious . . . mind your business!

MARCUS: *(Having a sudden realization.)* You were having sex!

ERICA: *(Startled by his bluntness, she speaks more loudly than she should at this hour of the night.)* Oh, my God! I can't believe you just said that!

MARCUS: Shhhhhh!! You'll wake them up! *(Continues to speak in a whisper.)* It's the only reason for why you were out so late. It's not that I even care . . . I could care less . . .

ERICA: *(A very loud whisper.)* For your information I was *not* having sex. What I do in my life is private!

MARCUS: Whatever. Wonder what Mom's gonna say when I tell her what time you came home.

ERICA: You wouldn't dare.

MARCUS: Oh I would. Unless you tell me where you were and then I won't say a word.

ERICA: You said you didn't care!

MARCUS: I'm just curious. It will be very fun to see how long they ground you for.

ERICA: No! I won't let you manipulate me — I'm not telling you!

MARCUS: OK. Let's see . . . I could tell Mom it was two-thirty when you came home, but I wonder what she'd do if I bumped it up to 4 AM?

ERICA: You little snitch! This is total blackmail!

MARCUS: *(Innocently.)* Is that what you call it?

ERICA: Look at you — you're gonna grow up to be a professional crook!

MARCUS: It's a good living.

ERICA: If I tell you — you promise you won't say anything?

MARCUS: My word of honor.

ERICA: Yeah, how much is that worth? You're a certified criminal.

MARCUS: I was goofin' on you — my word is good! I won't tell them! So where were you?

ERICA: *(She begins her "story" with MARCUS hanging on her every word.)* Well, we met this guy in front of 7-Eleven and he invited us to this party — some loft downtown — so we went. I'm pretty sure this guy deals drugs because there were tons of pills and powder everywhere. He asked me if I wanted to try some, so I thought OK, I'm young — gotta live a little! So I snorted this white powder and I felt so great and he told me I just snorted heroin. Then he asked me if I wanted to try smoking some crack and I said OK and that was amazing! It was all very cool.

MARCUS: *(Dumbfounded. After a beat he starts to speak.)* Oh, my God! Are you insane? Are you out of your mind? Do you have some death wish or something? You're high right now. I should have spotted it right away. You are a total dopehead!

ERICA: *(Bursting into laughter; he fell for her story hook, line, and sinker.)* Hahahahahaha! Gotcha! How does it feel to be conned, bro?

MARCUS: You mean . . . you were just kidding around? No drug dealers? No party? No heroin or crack?

ERICA: All just a figment of my amazing imagination! Joke's on you! Now if we're through here, I'm going to bed. In case you hadn't noticed, it's very late!

MARCUS: But you still didn't tell me where you were?

ERICA: And I never will little brother. Use *your* imagination! *(She starts to exit and calls back to him cheerfully.)* Good night!
(MARCUS is left alone looking very bewildered.)

END OF SCENE

FUNERAL FOR A FRIEND

As AUDREY and PATRICK prepare to attend a funeral for their friend Dean who died in a surfing accident, they reflect upon what they will miss most about him and how they will honor their memory of him.

AUDREY: You can't wear that!

PATRICK: Why not? What's wrong with it?

AUDREY: You can't wear board shorts to a funeral.

PATRICK: Why not? It's hot out.

AUDREY: It's disrespectful. You have to wear a suit.

PATRICK: Who made that rule?

AUDREY: It's common knowledge. Funerals are formal.

PATRICK: But why do they have to be? Dean wasn't a formal guy. He wouldn't have cared if I wore shorts to his funeral. Bet he would have liked it . . . would have wanted me to.

AUDREY: That's not the point.

PATRICK: Well, it should be. Why should I get all dressed up in uncomfortable clothes to say good-bye to a friend who probably never wore a suit in his entire life.

AUDREY: He's wearing one now.

PATRICK: And that sucks. They should've put him in his wet suit — that's what he was the most comfortable wearing. He totally would have dug that.

AUDREY: Yeah — he probably would have. God. I can't believe he's gone. I can't believe we're doing this — going to a funeral for a sixteen-year-old kid. It's not natural. Sixteen-year-olds aren't supposed to die.

PATRICK: I can't believe he's gone either. Yesterday I thought I saw him crossing the street. And then I saw some dude on a bike and he looked just like Dean. I'm seeing him everywhere — it's sorta freakin' me out.

AUDREY: I think it's cool. It's like he's still around — saying hi to you — making sure you won't forget him.

PATRICK: How could I ever forget him? We've been friends since . . . forever! He's the one who taught me to surf . . . showed me the way . . . taught me to not be afraid of the wave. Now I don't think I can ever get on a board again.

AUDREY: That's dumb. You have to. It would be like an insult to him if you stopped surfing.

PATRICK: But every time I go out there . . .

AUDREY: It'll be like he's riding with you. He shouldn't have died, Pat. It was a terrible accident. But at least he died doing exactly what he wanted to be doing.

PATRICK: That's true. He sure loved the water.

AUDREY: So you gotta keep his memory alive. And you can do that by doing what he loved best.

PATRICK: Riding the waves . . . very poetic.

AUDREY: It is. Come on, you know it is.

PATRICK: I'm still trying to make sense of all of it.

AUDREY: I don't think you can. It happened and there's nothing we can do to change that. We have to start accepting that.

PATRICK: We should get going, huh?

AUDREY: I guess you're not gonna change your clothes, are you?

PATRICK: I don't want to. And if I'm keeping Dean's memory alive, I need to wear this to say good-bye.

AUDREY: Yeah. I guess you're right. It's exactly what he would have wanted.

PATRICK: I think so too.

END OF SCENE

PERFECT CASTING

DUNCAN and COURTNEY used to date, but they are now broken up. They have just received the news that they will be playing the title roles in the school's upcoming production of Romeo and Juliet. *COURTNEY is concerned that the subject matter of the play and the nature of the roles will affect their broken-up status.*

DUNCAN: Cast list is up.

COURTNEY: Yeah, I know. I saw it.

DUNCAN: So, I guess — congratulations, right?

COURTNEY: Thanks. You too.

DUNCAN: I've been called Romeo three times already and the list only went up about a half hour ago.

COURTNEY: Well . . . get used to it, I guess.

DUNCAN: I didn't think I'd get it. Thought for sure it was gonna be Reed. You were a shoo-in though.

COURTNEY: Thanks. I think it was between me and Tanya Swenson. I saw her at the callback. She was really good.

DUNCAN: *(Sincerely.)* You'll make a much prettier Juliet.

COURTNEY: Cut it out, Duncan.

DUNCAN: What? I was complimenting you.

COURTNEY: It's gonna be hard enough getting through rehearsals and everything. Don't make it worse by . . .

DUNCAN: By what? I can't be nice to you? That's against the rules?

(COURTNEY doesn't answer.)

DUNCAN: Ya know, Court, it's only gonna be difficult if you make it difficult. I'm stoked I got the lead in this play. And just because we used to date . . . well that shouldn't have to get in the way of this being a great time. For both of us.

COURTNEY: We have to kiss.

DUNCAN: We do? Are you sure?

COURTNEY: Have you read the play? It's *Romeo and Juliet,* Duncan! They're in love with each other. They kiss.

DUNCAN: Well maybe they won't in this version of it. Maybe Mrs. Lerner won't stage it that way.

COURTNEY: Connie heard her talking to Mr. Gorman. She said, "My two leads have amazing chemistry. It's going to be a very romantic production."

DUNCAN: She said we had amazing chemistry? Cool. Do you think Mrs. L knows we used to date?

COURTNEY: I don't know. But she sure saw something between us during the audition.

DUNCAN: Sparks *were* flying, Court. No denying that. There *is* something between us. Always will be.

COURTNEY: Look, Duncan, I don't want to get back together with you. We'll just starting fighting again, like before and you'll start looking at other girls like before, and it's not worth it. Maybe we do have chemistry — but I'm not sure we're meant to be together. I can't go through all that again. It's gonna be so hard doing this play with you — having to be in love with you — I don't know *what's* going to happen.

DUNCAN: Do you want me to drop out? If I do, Mrs. L will probably give the part to Reed.

COURTNEY: You would do that?

DUNCAN: I don't want to, Court. I really want to play this part. But if you're gonna get all tweaked about it . . . I don't know . . . maybe it's *not* worth it.

COURTNEY: That is the sweetest, most generous thing you've ever said to me.

DUNCAN: Well I'm not a bad guy, ya know! I think we would be great together. Onstage, I mean. I'm not talking about getting back together . . . although . . .

COURTNEY: If I have to kiss Romeo, I'd much rather kiss you than Reed Chambers.

DUNCAN: Good! So we're all good then? No one's dropping out of the play? You're not gonna tweak out on me?

COURTNEY: You *would* be the better Romeo. It's not fair to make you drop out because of our personal issues. I'll try to be professional about the whole thing. It is pretty exciting that out of everyone who auditioned, you and I are playing Romeo and Juliet.

DUNCAN: It's fate, babe.

COURTNEY: Yeah! Being star-crossed lovers is our destiny.

DUNCAN: Doesn't have to be, Court. We can change our destiny, ya know.

COURTNEY: Let's just show up to rehearsal and see what happens, OK?

DUNCAN: So we're not ruling anything out then, right?

COURTNEY: Don't push me, Duncan. Let's just see what happens, Romeo, O Romeo!

DUNCAN: Whatever your lovely heart desires my fair maiden, my Juliet.

(He gently brushes his hand against her cheek — getting into character.)

COURTNEY: *(Enjoying the attention but not wanting to show it.)* Oh brother . . . let's not get carried away, OK? Save the romance for rehearsal.

END OF SCENE

AT THE MOVIES

PAIGE and RILEY are waiting in line for a highly anticipated blockbuster movie that just opened the day before. PAIGE becomes upset when she finds out RILEY has already seen the movie without her.

PAIGE: Look at this line! I've never seen this theater so crowded!

RILEY: It's a huge movie. Everyone's talking about it.

PAIGE: I can't wait!

RILEY: It's so awesome.

PAIGE: What is?

RILEY: The movie.

PAIGE: How do you know?

RILEY: *(Trying to cover up.)* I mean . . . it's *going* to be so awesome.

PAIGE: Riley, did you see it already?

RILEY: What?

PAIGE: This movie? Did you already see it?

RILEY: *(Hesitantly.)* Kind of?

PAIGE: *(She starts speaking a little louder making RILEY self-conscious.)* What do you mean "kind of"? You either saw it or you didn't.

RILEY: Could you please lower your voice. People are starting to stare.

PAIGE: Let them stare . . . I don't care. Riley, would you please answer my question.

RILEY: *(Stalling.)* Uh . . . what was the question again?

PAIGE: *(Frustrated.)* Oh! I'm going to kill you! You saw this already! You promised me you'd take me to see it when it came out!

RILEY: And I am taking you. We're here.

PAIGE: But you saw it already. When did you see it? It just opened!

RILEY: Yesterday. I saw it yesterday. I'm sorry but I love

seeing movies on opening day. You were busy, so I went without you. I knew we'd be seeing it together tonight.

PAIGE: You couldn't wait one stinking day?! What's wrong with you?

RILEY: It's a tradition I have with myself. But don't be mad, babe — we're seeing it together. We're here now.

PAIGE: It's not the same thing.

RILEY: Why not?

PAIGE: Well, I have my own tradition. I hate going to the movies with someone who's already seen the movie and I haven't. I want it to be fresh — for both of us. And you just saw it *yesterday!* It is *so* not fresh for you.

RILEY: But I don't mind. You know I love seeing movies over and over again.

PAIGE: But I wanted the first time to be with me! Who'd you go with anyway?

RILEY: My sister. My mom made me take her when she found out I was going.

PAIGE: Did she like it?

RILEY: She loved it. She's going to see it again tomorrow with her friends.

PAIGE: What is with your family? If you're going to see a movie more than once, you should at least wait a week. Get a breather.

RILEY: What can I say? We like repetition.

PAIGE: So . . . it's really, really good?

RILEY: You're gonna love it. It's awesome.

PAIGE: And you're not gonna whisper in my ear through the whole thing? You won't ruin it for me?

RILEY: I'll stop talking the minute the lights go out. I won't even say anything during the coming attractions. It'll be like I'm seeing it for the first time. With you.

PAIGE: Well . . . I'm still pretty mad at you for doing this. But . . . I'm definitely not leaving now. Don't do it again, OK?

RILEY: Hey, I can promise you a lot, but I can't promise that

I'll stop going to see movies on opening day. It's just this thing I have.

PAIGE: You're weird.

RILEY: I know. What can I say?

PAIGE: Oh, finally. The line's moving. Hey you get the popcorn and I'll find seats, OK?

RILEY: Yeah. And tomorrow? If you're not doing anything? Ya wanna go to the movies again?

PAIGE: And see what?

RILEY: This! I'm telling you, you're gonna want to see it again.

PAIGE: Let me just enjoy seeing it the first time, Ri, before I make any future plans OK?

RILEY: Well, wait and see. You're gonna die when you see the part where the guy . . .

PAIGE: *(Interrupting.)* Hey, hey! Shush! You said you weren't gonna give anything away! You really want to see this movie three days in a row? I think I'm dating a geek!

END OF SCENE

FLORENCE NIGHTINGALE

ANNA *visits her boyfriend STUART at home and finds him in bed with a very bad cold. She is anxious to play "nurse" and wants to help him feel better, but all STUART wants is to be left alone. He tries very hard not to hurt her feelings, but her pushiness sends him over the edge.*

ANNA: *(Upon entering, she sees how sick STUART really is as he lies in bed.)* Oh, my God . . . Your mom told me you were sick but I thought you were secretly faking.

STUART: *(With a stuffed nose.)* I'm not faking.

ANNA: I can see that! Poor baby . . . do you have a fever?

STUART: I dunno. I think so. I'm all achy.

ANNA: Ohhhh . . . Do you have chills? Put this blanket over you. *(She pulls the blanket over STUART and proceeds to tuck him in.)*

STUART: *(Kicking the blanket off immediately.)* No . . . I get too hot.

ANNA: *(Putting the blanket back on him patiently.)* But that's good. You have to sweat it out.

STUART: *(Kicking the blanket off once again, he answers her harshly.)* NO! It's too hot! I'm uncomfortable. Just leave me be, OK?

ANNA: *(Hurt.)* I'm just trying to help.

STUART: *(Softening.)* I know. I know. But I'm sick . . . and I kinda want to be left alone right now, OK?

ANNA: *(Not taking the hint.)* Well . . . do you want me to read to you? I can read you the English assignment so you won't get behind in class?

STUART: *(Impatiently.)* No . . . *please* don't read to me! I just need to get some rest.

ANNA: So rest! I'll just sit here and keep you company. I can go get us a DVD? How about we watch a movie together? Would that be good?

STUART: I know you're trying to help and I appreciate it; I really do. But I think it's probably a good idea if you left now. So I can hurry up and get better.

ANNA: Oh, you don't want to be alone, silly! No one wants to be alone when they're sick.

STUART: I do! I *really* do! I like to suffer in silence.

ANNA: But there's no reason to suffer . . . I can get you anything you want. Anything you need. Oh! You know what would be good for you? Chicken soup! I'll run to the deli and pick up some chicken noodle soup for you.

STUART: *(Muttering to himself.)* I'm in hell. You're worse than my mother!

ANNA: *(Oblivious.)* So I'll get you some?

STUART: *(Starts building to where he's yelling at her by the end.)* Look Anna, honey, I appreciate everything you're trying to do . . . but I don't want any soup. I don't want you to read to me. I don't want to watch a movie and I don't want the blanket on me. *I want to be left alone.*

ANNA: *(Shocked at his outburst.)* Well . . . you don't have to be so rude about it, Stuart! I know you don't feel well but that's no excuse for biting my head off!

STUART: *(Exhausted.)* I'm sorry. I'm sorry. I'm sorry! Pleeeeeaaaaasssseeeee . . . you're killin' me! Don't you like to be left alone when you're sick?

ANNA: *(Haughtily.)* As a matter of fact . . . no! I *like* the extra attention. I like being pampered when I feel bad. I just want to help you get better. But if you want me to leave . . . I guess I can take a hint.

STUART: *(Relieved.)* Thank you.

(She starts to leave and he calls out to her.)

STUART: Don't be mad!

ANNA: *(Steps back into the room.)* I'm not mad. I just think you could be a little more considerate! Here I am, trying to help you and you're kicking me out!

STUART: *(He completely loses it so by the end of his speech his emotional outburst has caused him to have a coughing attack.)* You want *me* to be considerate of *you!* I'm the one who's sick! You're supposed to be considering *my* feelings. But you can't take a hint. You just keep flitting about and all I want is for you to go home so that I can get some sleep! *(Begins coughing uncontrollably. ANNA doesn't seem to have any compassion.)*

ANNA: Calm down. Don't go getting all riled up — you're gonna cough up a lung.

STUART: *(In between coughs.)* You're the one who riled me up! I get *no* rest if you're around.

ANNA: OK. Fine. I said I'd leave. So I'm leaving. Go to sleep. Go get well. We'll talk when you're better.

STUART: *(His coughing has begun to subside.)* Thank you. Oh man, I think I broke a rib.

ANNA: That's what you get for getting so worked up over nothing.

STUART: Right. Nothing. OK. So I'll call you later.

ANNA: Only if you're feeling up to it. You see? I'm a very understanding person. You want to be alone — I'll leave you alone! I'd make a great nurse.

STUART: *(Exhausted from this entire confrontation.)* Well actually, you're a little pushy to be a nurse. You're definitely no Florence Nightingale!

(Without waiting for ANNA to respond, STUART rolls over and goes to sleep.)

END OF SCENE

Scenes for Three or More

MR. RIGHT

3 Females/1 Male

KENDRA, MARIE, and TINA are meeting at 31 Flavors because TINA has a crush on EVAN, the boy who works there. Things do not go the way TINA hoped they would, and together, with her friends, they make plans to help her find "Mr. Right."

MARIE: What time did she tell you to meet her here?

KENDRA: She said she'd be here by seven. She'd better come because I won't have a ride home otherwise.

MARIE: She'll be here. She's in love with Evan and he's working tonight. Believe me, she'll be here. Come on, let's go in. *(They enter the store. EVAN is working behind the counter. There is no one else in the shop.)*

EVAN: Hello ladies!

MARIE: Hi, Ev . . . slow tonight, huh?

EVAN: It's fine with me . . . I hate working here. The less I have to do the better.

KENDRA: *(Flirtatiously.)* What a slacker!

EVAN: Least I have a job . . . more than I can say for a lot of kids . . .

MARIE: That's true.

(TINA quickly walks into the store, eyeing EVAN the entire time she is speaking with the other girls.)

TINA: Hi, girls . . . Sorry I'm late. I couldn't find a place to park. *(Looks directly at EVAN as if she's noticing him for the first time.)* Oh, hi, Evan.

EVAN: Hey, how's it going? You couldn't find parking? Really? It's dead down here tonight.

TINA: Everyone's probably at the movies. You're gonna be busy later when the movie gets out.

EVAN: *(Sarcastically.)* Great. I'm looking forward to it.

KENDRA: *(To TINA.)* You're giving me a ride home, right? You said you would.

TINA: *(Distracted.)* Yeah, I'll give you a lift. Whatever . . .

MARIE: So what do you want to do? I don't have to be home until eleven.

KENDRA: I wanna check out that new shoe store down the street. They're supposed to have designer shoes for half price.

EVAN: So, ladies . . . is this just a gathering place or can I scoop you some ice cream?

TINA: Oh . . . no ice cream for me. I'm off sugar and dairy.

EVAN: What about you, Kendra? Are you off sugar too?

KENDRA: *(Surprised by his attention.)* What? Oh. No. I'd love a pralines and cream . . . *(Notices TINA glaring at her.)* But I probably shouldn't.

EVAN: Oh come on! It's on the house. You don't need to worry about what you eat. You look great!

KENDRA: Wow! OK. Thanks.

TINA: Well maybe I *will* have one, Evan. I mean, ya gotta live a little right?

EVAN: Yeah. Right. Whatever.

MARIE: Tina, come here for a second. I have to show you something.

TINA: Let me get my ice cream first.

MARIE: No. Come here first. It's important.

(KENDRA moves closer to the counter to talk to EVAN. MARIE and TINA whisper in the corner.)

MARIE: You told me to let you know if you started acting like a jerk in front of him. Well guess what? You're approaching jerklike behavior.

TINA: I am not! He's giving me free ice cream!

MARIE: I hate to break your heart, but it seems really obvious that he likes Kendra. He's totally flirting with her.

EVAN: Hey, Tina, what flavor did you want?

TINA: What do you suggest?

EVAN: I don't know. What do you like?

TINA: *(Whispering to MARIE.)* See, he wants to know what I like!

MARIE: You are really reaching.

EVAN: Uh . . . hello . . . do you want one or not?

KENDRA: *(Eating her cone.)* The pralines and cream is really good.

TINA: OK. Pralines and cream. I'll have that.

EVAN: Hey, Kendra, come here. No . . . closer . . . you got a little ice cream on your face. Let me wipe it off for you. *(He wipes her face with a napkin, KENDRA becomes flustered.)*

KENDRA: Oh . . . hey . . . I can do it. *(She takes the napkin away from him as she becomes aware TINA is watching their every move.)*

EVAN: So . . . I heard you say you needed a ride home.

KENDRA: Well, Tina's gonna take me.

EVAN: I can take you. I'm out of here by ten. Meet me back here and I'll take you home.

TINA: *(Desperately.)* No! I mean, she has to come with me.

EVAN/KENDRA: Why?

TINA: Uh . . . because I told her mom *I'd* bring her home.

KENDRA: No, you didn't. As long as I get a ride from someone it doesn't matter. I just don't want to be stuck down here.

MARIE: *(Taking charge.)* You're taking *me* home, Tina. Let Evan take Kendra.

TINA: But . . .

EVAN: Cool. So come back here at ten, OK?

KENDRA: Yeah. OK. Thanks for the ice cream.

EVAN: You are more than welcome.

TINA: *(Her last attempt to get him to notice her.)* Yeah. Thanks for the cone, Evan. It's delicious.

EVAN: Uh-huh.

(The three girls exit the store.)

TINA: *(To KENDRA.)* I can't believe you did that to me.

KENDRA: I didn't *do* anything. He came on to me.

TINA: *(To MARIE.)* Did you see how she totally betrayed me?

MARIE: Come on, Tina . . . be fair. Evan's into her; it's not her fault.

TINA: Well you didn't have to accept a ride home from him.

KENDRA: Are you kidding? He's hot. Look, he came after me. I'm not going to ignore him.

MARIE: Seriously Tina, if the shoe was on the other foot, wouldn't you do the same thing?

TINA: No! I wouldn't betray a friend. If I knew you liked a guy I wouldn't go near him.

MARIE: I don't think that's true.

KENDRA: Me neither.

TINA: Well thanks a lot you two — I thought I could trust you both.

MARIE: Tina, stop getting so upset. You didn't even know if Evan liked you. Now you know the truth. I've got a great idea. Let's go over to Starbucks. There's that really cute guy working over there. Evan chose Kendra, so now it's time for you to move on to the next.

TINA: You mean that guy; I think his name is Thomas? He's really cute. OK, let's go over there. But Kendra, you stay here. I don't need you stealing another guy away from me.

KENDRA: Fine with me. I'll just keep Evan company till it's time to go home.

TINA: Let's go. And Marie — don't *you* get any ideas either. Let me do all the talking.

MARIE: Hey, Thomas is all yours. He's cute, but he's not my type.

TINA: Good! Maybe he'll turn out to be Mr. Right. Because I really need to get a boyfriend!

MARIE: Hey, you don't *need* a boyfriend. You're fine without one!

TINA: I know. I know. But it sure would be nice to have one, don't you think?

KENDRA: Amen!

END OF SCENE

A NIGHT TO REMEMBER

3 Males

After a party at a friend's house, NOAH and IAN try to rouse their buddy GAVIN who drank too much beer and has passed out cold.

NOAH: What are we gonna do? We can't leave him here.

IAN: What's wrong with him?

NOAH: I don't know. He's sleeping, I guess.

IAN: He's not sleeping. He's passed out!

NOAH: What's the difference?

IAN: The difference is that he was drinking all night long and now we can't even get him to move. Oh man, he is so in for it.

NOAH: Well, we need to *try* and get him up. I've gotta bring him home.

IAN: If we bring him home like this, we'll never see him again. His parents will freak! They'll send him off to military school or something.

NOAH: What was he drinking?

IAN: Beer, man. It was everywhere. They had kegs set up *everywhere*. Even in the bathroom, like I would drink *that!* Didn't you have some?

NOAH: No. Believe it or not, I'm really not into drinking. Doesn't really do it for me, ya know? Who brought in beer anyway?

IAN: I think Nelson's older brother got it. Their parents don't come home till Sunday. Look at this place! Sure glad it's not my house — I'd hate to have to clean this mess up.

NOAH: Let's try to wake him up.

IAN: I could throw some cold water on him.

NOAH: No man, don't do that. Just slap him.

IAN: *You* slap him! I don't want to get punched in the face!

NOAH: Fine. I'll do it. *(Standing over GAVIN.)* Well, here goes . . . *(He starts slapping him gently across the face.)* Gav . . . Gavin . . . C'mon man, wake up!
(GAVIN doesn't move.)

IAN: You gotta do it harder than that — you're hittin' him like he's a little girl. He's never gonna wake up at this rate. I'm gonna get some cold water to throw on him.

NOAH: Wait, wait, wait! Let me try it one more time! *(NOAH starts shaking GAVIN and slapping him a little harder. After no movement, he screams directly into his face.)* GAAAAA-VINNNNNNN!!!!

GAVIN: *(Starts to move slowly and begins to moan. Sees NOAH and smiles drunkenly.)* Hey, Stink . . . pull the car over will ya? I think I'm gonna puke.

IAN: Hate to tell you brother, you're not *in* a car. You're not even moving.

GAVIN: Oh yes I am. Oh, man . . . I'm gonna be sick.
(He rolls over and vomits loudly.)

NOAH: Oh this is great! Just great!

IAN: Well it's better than having him puke in your car.

NOAH: Who's gonna clean that up? Man, it reeks!

IAN: Nelson is. His party. His house. His cleanup.

NOAH: That's just wrong.

IAN: Then you clean it up.

GAVIN: *(Sitting up and looking around dazed.)* Hey! What happened?

NOAH: Looks like you can't hold your beer, Gav. How much did you drink anyway?

GAVIN: *(Holding his head — trying to remember.)* I don't know. Last thing I remember I was chattin' up Cindy Harris . . . can't really remember if I asked her out or not. I think I did. I think she even said yes. Ah crap . . . I can't remember a thing. Hey where is everybody anyway?

IAN: Sleepin'. Passed out. Most people left hours ago. We were waiting on you. It was a great party — for a little while anyway.

GAVIN: What time is it? I gotta get home. My parents are gonna kill me.

NOAH: If they see you like this, are they gonna send you away? Like to military school or something?

GAVIN: Yeah! Probably.

IAN: *(To NATHAN.)* Told ya. *(To GAVIN.)* Hey, are you sober enough to face them?

GAVIN: Let me just go and splash some cold water on my face. *(He slowly starts to rise to his feet. He's very unsteady.)*

IAN: See! I knew we should've thrown water on him.

GAVIN: Hey, you guys? Did I do anything . . . ya know . . . weird tonight? Something I'm gonna regret if I only I could remember what it was?

NOAH: You mean did you dance with a lampshade or your head or something like that?

GAVIN: Did I?

IAN: Yeah! You asked Cindy Harris out! What were you thinking? Aarf aarf!

NOAH: Hey cut it out. She's OK.

GAVIN: She's no dog. You're the dog. You couldn't even ask out a dog!

IAN: I'll have you know that I got quite a few phone numbers tonight.

NOAH: Yeah? From who? The pizza-delivery guy?

IAN: Very funny. I'll have you know . . .

GAVIN: *(Interrupting.)* Hey, guys . . . as much as I'd love to stay and reminiscence about the fun we had tonight, I gotta get home . . . oh, boy . . . but first . . . oh, boy . . . I think I'm gonna be sick again.

NOAH: Well try to make it to the bathroom this time, would you? And make sure you get it *all* out of your system 'cause I don't want you puking in my car — I just washed it!

GAVIN: Oh, God . . . *(He runs out of the room.)*

IAN: He's dead. His parents take one look at that green face of his and he is dead in the water.

NOAH: He can always say he got food poisoning.

IAN: Yeah, beer's a food, isn't it?

NOAH: We better say our good-byes tonight.

IAN: What do you mean?

NOAH: I mean that Gavin's gonna be pretty busy tomorrow packing his bags. Looks like that boy is going to military school!

END OF SCENE

CONFRONTING THE OBVIOUS

3 Females

*RENE and GINA are concerned about their friend
VANESSA'S health and suspect that she may be bulimic.
When they decide to confront her, they are surprised at
how angry she becomes.*

RENE: She's in there again.

GINA: Again? She went to the bathroom *again?!*

RENE: I think we should say something.

GINA: Does she really think that we don't know? It's so obvious.

RENE: And it's getting worse, don't you think? All the signs
are there, G; we have to do something.

GINA: What? She can't feel like we're ganging up on her.

RENE: Of course not. We just need to bring it up gently.

GINA: Bring it up? That's pretty funny.

RENE: You're sick. You know what I mean.

GINA: Here she comes . . . you do it. I have no idea what to
say to her.

RENE: Oh thanks. I'm the bad guy. Vanessa, hey! We're over
here.

VANESSA: Hey, Gina! You just get here? That's such a cute
shirt, is it new?

GINA: Kind of. I've worn it a couple of times. You can borrow it if you want.

VANESSA: Are you kidding? You're so much smaller than
me . . . it would never fit.

RENE: Uh . . . you're looking pretty small these days,
Vanessa . . . I think you've lost a lot of weight.

VANESSA: No I haven't. It's all an illusion. Wearing black all
the time makes me look thinner.

GINA: I think you look smaller too. This shirt would definitely
fit you.

VANESSA: Well, thanks. Maybe I'll try it on later, OK? So what's the plan?

RENE: Before we decide that, I uh . . . I wanted to ask you if you've been . . . um . . . if you've been feeling OK?

VANESSA: What are you talking about?

RENE: Well, I couldn't help but notice that the past few weeks, you're like *always* in the bathroom?

VANESSA: So? I have a small bladder. I drink a lot of water.

GINA: And you really do look a lot thinner, Nessa. Are you sure everything is OK?

VANESSA: I can't seem to get rid of this stomach flu, that's all. I guess I've dropped a few pounds, but it's only water weight. I'm fine, girls! No need to worry.

RENE: But Vanessa, when you were at my house the other day — you were in the bathroom for like a really long time.

GINA: And just now — you were in there for quite awhile.

VANESSA: What are you guys doing? Timing me? Is there now a time limit for bathroom use that I'm not aware of? What is your problem? Is this some kind of joke?

RENE: Please don't get upset. We're worried about you, that's all.

VANESSA: *(Getting increasingly more defensive.)* I'm fine! There's nothing to worry about. Get a life, ya know? Stop monitoring my bathroom habits.

GINA: Nessa, you have to admit it all looks very suspicious.

VANESSA: What? What looks suspicious?

RENE: Gina, don't.

GINA: No! We need to say something. You're in the bathroom *all the time* with the "stomach flu." You're losing weight. Now you're getting all defensive. We think you're making yourself throw up. That's why we're worried. Stop acting like you don't know what we're talking about.

VANESSA: What the hell is going on with everybody? Have you two been talking to my mother?

RENE: So she thinks there's something wrong too?

VANESSA: Nothing is wrong! God! I feel like no one is

hearing me! I'm sorry if I have to use the bathroom so often. I'm sorry if that bothers the two of you. I am not some charity case — some "cause." Some broke thing that needs fixing — -*Rene!* You're always trying to fix things. Well, don't fix me! I'm saying this for the last time. *I'm fine!* If you don't believe me there's nothing I can do about it.

GINA: You are so totally in denial.

VANESSA: No Gina, *you* are! If you want drama, then you go be the bulimic! I don't know what else to say to you.

RENE: We didn't mean to make you mad, Van. It just seems like you've had this flu for a really long time. Maybe you should go to the doctor.

VANESSA: And maybe you both need to stay out of my business.

GINA: We're just trying to help! We care about you!

VANESSA: You want to help? Stay out of my life!

RENE: Vanessa . . . come on . . . don't be like that. Don't walk away mad.

VANESSA: How would you like it if I started prying into your most private moments? How about you, Gina? How would you like it if I put my ear to the door every time you went to the bathroom?

GINA: I never did that! I never put my ear to the door.

VANESSA: Whatever! Just do me a favor: *Leave me alone!* That's how you can help. *(She angrily walks away from them.)*

GINA: Wow. We really blew it.

RENE: Maybe we *are* wrong. God, I can't believe how mad she got.

GINA: That's exactly why we're not wrong. If she weren't bulimic, she wouldn't have gotten so incredibly defensive. This clinches it.

RENE: So what do we do? Should we go talk to her mom?

GINA: She's gonna kill us if we do.

RENE: And the bulimia is gonna kill her.

GINA: You can't die from that.

RENE: Yes you can. I'm pretty sure you can. You can get really sick anyway. They'd have to put her in the hospital. She doesn't even see how thin she is. She thought your shirt was too small for her. We definitely have to tell her mother.

GINA: Well, I'm all for helping Vanessa and everything. I just hope we don't make things worse than they already are.

RENE: She's already mad at us. Might as well go all that way.

GINA: You're right. Let's do it. Let's go call her mom.

END OF SCENE

OBJECT OF DESIRE

2 Males/1 Female

After the mother of one of their friends has plastic surgery, JACK and GARY become obsessed with her sudden, stunning beauty. They tell their friend CLAUDIA about the newly transformed woman and how they feel about the possibility of dating an older woman.

JACK: *(To GARY.)* So? Did you see her?

CLAUDIA: See who? Who are you talking about?

JACK: *(Ignoring CLAUDIA.)* Did you?

GARY: Yup. I saw her. You're totally right.

CLAUDIA: Who are you talking about?

JACK: Should we tell her?

GARY: She'll think we're pigs.

CLAUDIA: Please stop talking about me like I'm not here and just tell me who you're talking about.

GARY: Sorry.

CLAUDIA: Are you gonna tell me?

JACK: Ritchie Caldwell's mom.

CLAUDIA: What about her?

GARY: Have you seen her recently?

CLAUDIA: No. I don't know. I'm not really friends with Richard. What's the big deal?

JACK: Well . . . she is . . . something else. Unbelievable.

GARY: She sure is.

CLAUDIA: What does that mean, "she's something else"? Would you guys just tell me what you're talking about?

JACK: Well it seems Mrs. Caldwell had some work done. Some botox. And a little lift here and a little lift there.

GARY: *(Singing to the tune of "Old McDonald Had a Farm.")* Here a lift, there a lift, everywhere a lift, lift.

CLAUDIA: She had plastic surgery? So what? Everybody's doing it these days.

JACK: Well, she had some great surgeon, I'll tell you that.

GARY: She is soooo hot!

CLAUDIA: Richard Caldwell's mom is *hot?* You guys *are* pigs!

GARY: You don't understand. I guess she was always an attractive woman, but now . . . I'm not exactly sure what she did, but holy moly! She could be Ritchie's older sister.

JACK: Can you imagine having a mother that looks like that?

CLAUDIA: I would hate it.

JACK: Well, of course, *you* would hate it. You're a girl. She'd be competition for you.

CLAUDIA: Hey!

GARY: He's got a point. No girl wants her mother to be hotter than she is. But I don't think I'd want my mom to look like that either. Guys coming over to my house all the time just to sneak a peek of my *mother!* Something a little bit creepy about that.

CLAUDIA: Have you said anything to Richard? Did you tell him that you're into his mom?

JACK: Ritchie's clueless. He has no idea. But mama mia . . . I would ask her out in a second.

CLAUDIA: Jack! That's sick. You want to date someone the same age as your mom?

JACK: Why not? She looks amazing. She's got the flattest stomach and the tightest butt.

CLAUDIA: OK, OK, I get the picture. You sure did get a good look didn't you?

JACK: I couldn't help myself. But she was also wearing some pretty tight clothes — showing off I guess.

GARY: She definitely has a lot to be proud of. What a woman!

CLAUDIA: You guys are totally gaga over her . . . I've never seen you like this before.

JACK: Well, ya know what they say about older women . . .

CLAUDIA: What? What do they say? I'd like to hear this!

JACK: With age comes wisdom . . .

GARY: Oh yeah. I get it. She could teach us the ways of the world.

JACK: And how!

CLAUDIA: *(Rolling her eyes, exasperated with the boys.)* Aren't you guys forgetting about one little thing?

GARY: What?

CLAUDIA: Mr. Caldwell.

GARY: Oh yeah. Wait! *Is* there a Mr. Caldwell?

JACK: That's a good question. I don't know. I can't remember if Ritchie has ever mentioned his dad or not.

GARY: Maybe that's why she got the plastic surgery. She's a single woman looking to get some action.

CLAUDIA: Or maybe it has nothing to do with a man and she just wanted to feel better about herself. Did that ever occur to you two boneheads?

GARY: Why else would you get all that work done? You want to look hot for the opposite sex.

CLAUDIA: You just don't understand a thing about women.

GARY: So enlighten me!

JACK: See, that's why we need to date Mrs. Caldwell. She'd be like our mentor.

CLAUDIA: As if she would be interested in a couple of hyper, smelly, immature teenage boys.

JACK: We don't smell. You never said anything about us smelling before.

GARY: I take very good care of my personal hygiene thank you very much. Maybe not so much in eighth grade, but I'm much better about it now!

CLAUDIA: Well assuming there is no Mr. Caldwell, which you don't know for sure anyway, I don't think either one of you has a chance in hell in dating an older woman. You both need to grow up a little bit. You need to grow up *a lot*! You wouldn't be able to handle it.

JACK: *(Winking at GARY.)* Maybe *she* wouldn't be able to handle *us*!

GARY: Yeah! Ever think of that?

CLAUDIA: Oh right! In your dreams.

JACK: *(Nodding his head.)* Oh yes! Every night. I'll be seeing her there every single night!

CLAUDIA: That's gross.

GARY: I think it's love.

JACK: Hey c'mon, Gare, let's not get carried away.

CLAUDIA: Lust then! It's lust! And you need to get over it because she's never gonna date a pimply-faced little boy like you.

JACK: *(Pretending to be hurt.)* How dare you! You're a very cruel person, Claudia.

CLAUDIA: I just wouldn't want you to get your hopes up.

GARY: Ya never know, Claud. Stranger things have happened.

CLAUDIA: A lot stranger. Trust me, *this* isn't going to happen. I'd bet on it.

END OF SCENE

SURPRISE PARTY

2 Females/1 Male

LEXI and ETHAN are throwing a surprise party for their friend DANA'S birthday. However, everyone seems to be doing too good a job of keeping the surprise because DANA has the feeling that all her friends not only forgot her birthday, but they also seem to want nothing do with her.

LEXI: Is everything ready? All the details in place?

ETHAN: Yup. Everyone knows — they'll all be at your house at seven.

LEXI: No one can show up late — they have to be there no later than seven; otherwise, she's gonna see people and it'll totally ruin everything.

ETHAN: Relax, Lex. Everyone knows they can't be late. It'll go smoothly. I'm sure it will. It will be the best surprise party you've ever thrown.

LEXI: It's the first surprise party I've ever thrown. Must be why I'm so nervous. Do you think Dana suspects anything?

ETHAN: I'm almost positive she doesn't. And if she does, she's a really good actress cause she's acting all bummed and everything.

LEXI: It's her birthday. What's she bummed about?

ETHAN: Everyone is keeping the surprise party such a great secret and they're all being so careful not to give anything away. They're being *so* careful that no one has even wished her happy birthday. I guess she thinks we all forgot.

LEXI: Well that's no good.

ETHAN: No one wants to blow the surprise.

LEXI: Well they're not gonna ruin the surprise by saying happy birthday. Ignoring her will make her just as suspicious that something's up.

ETHAN: Here she comes. Don't say anything about anything!

LEXI: I'm gonna wish her a happy birthday at least.

ETHAN: But . . .

(DANA approaches. ETHAN abruptly stops talking.)

DANA: Hey you guys . . . what're you doing?

LEXI: Hey Dana! *(She goes to give her a hug.)* Happy birthday, honey-pie!

DANA: *(Glumly.)* Oh. Thanks. You know you're the first and *only* person to say anything to me. *(Pointing an accusing finger at ETHAN.)* Even *he* didn't remember what today was!

ETHAN: I did too remember. How could I forget when you constantly reminded me every day for an entire week?

DANA: You didn't say *anything.* You picked me up this morning and acted like it was just . . . ya know . . . an average day.

ETHAN: It *is* an average day.

DANA: Oh, thanks. I can see I really mean a lot to you. This day sucks!

LEXI: Hey cut it out, you two. No fighting! The day's not over yet, Dana. I'm sure it'll get better.

DANA: I don't know what's wrong with everyone. People are acting like they're mad at me or something. I almost feel like people are ignoring me. It's weird. No one has said anything to me . . . I'm not just talking about saying happy birthday, no one has even said hi or good morning. I feel like a leper. They look at me and then they look away really fast. It's freakin' me out.

ETHAN: What exactly do you want to happen anyway? You want trumpets to blast? Balloons to fall from the sky? For everyone else, it's just a regular day. We have to go to school. We have to take tests. We have to eat lunch. The world doesn't stop just because today is Dana's birthday.

DANA: *(To LEXI.)* Do you see what I mean? *(To ETHAN.)* Why are you being such a jerk about this? Are you mad at me? Are you mad because I happen to want a little extra attention today? Pardon me for having a birthday and wanting to have a good day.

LEXI: *(Giving ETHAN a dirty look.)* Yeah Ethan, you are being a bit *harsh*. What bug crawled up your butt? Dana has every right to want balloons to fall from the sky. You wanted special treatment on your birthday. Everyone does. *(Turning her attention to DANA.)* I'm sorry you're having such a rotten day, D.

DANA: I guess it doesn't matter. Or it shouldn't matter. Birthdays are stupid anyway once you get older. What did I expect? My mom would come to school and hand out cupcakes and everybody would sing to me in homeroom? I'm just being dumb. I'm sorry, you guys. I'm being really childish. It's not like I wanted tons of presents or anything. But it would have been nice to have it acknowledged at least.

ETHAN: *(Full of guilt, he blurts out the following.)* Oh, God . . . I'm sorry, babe. I don't want you to feel sad. And I'm sorry I didn't say anything to you this morning . . . I guess I just have a lot on my mind. I've got so much work to do before the party tonight, and I'm kinda freakin' out because I don't know if I'll get it all done in time.

LEXI: *Ethan!*

DANA: Party? What party?

LEXI: *(Completely disgusted.)* You blew it! You totally blew it!

ETHAN: *(Realizing that he has let the cat out of the bag.)* Oh God! Lexi — don't kill me. I can't believe it; it just fell out of my mouth before I could stop myself. I'm so sorry. Oh man, I am more than sorry. Lexi, stop looking at me like that — it was an accident. I'm just not good at keeping secrets. Dana, promise me you'll act surprised.

DANA: *(Delighted.)* A surprise party? Is that what's going on?

LEXI: Oh Dana . . . Ethan ruined it! It's been planned for weeks, and I really thought we could pull it off. I feel so bad that you're having such a rotten day, but I know we'll all make it up to you tonight at the party. It's going to be fantastic!

(To ETHAN.) I can't believe you just blurted it out — you're such a dumb ass!

DANA: You guys! I can't believe you two — this is so cool. Now I feel totally stupid — I thought you all had abandoned me. I even thought my mom forgot. This is so great. So when is it? And where is it? And who's coming?

ETHAN: Well it's tonight at seven and I'm supposed to pretend that I'm . . .

LEXI: *Ethan!* Shut up! You've already ruined the initial surprise; you don't have to tell her every single detail, do you? Let some things be a secret.

ETHAN: You're right. I'm sorry. Screwed up again. I can't help it. This is a lot of pressure!

LEXI: Dana, I feel terrible . . .

DANA: Don't. I'm so relieved. I thought I was going crazy. I thought everyone hated me. This is the nicest thing anyone has ever done for me. I love you guys. Thank you *so* much!

LEXI: Promise me that you'll act surprised, OK? I don't want to tell everyone Ethan screwed up and let the secret out and that you actually knew about this all along.

ETHAN: You're never gonna let me live this down, are you?

LEXI: No. I'm not.

ETHAN: *(To DANA.)* I'm sorry, Boo. Sorry I messed up your birthday surprise.

LEXI: But we've got a lot more surprises in store so don't worry. Just don't tell her about anything else, Ethan!

DANA: Ethan, it's fine. Don't worry about it. I'm glad I found out this way. It's gonna make the rest of the day bearable. Now I have something to look forward to.

ETHAN: See, she forgives me.

LEXI: She's a nicer person than I am.

ETHAN: That's for sure.

DANA: Hey! Now you two stop fighting. I don't want anything else to ruin today! It's my birthday, damn it, and we're gonna have fun!

LEXI: Yes we are! But stop looking so happy. Keep pretending to be depressed, otherwise everyone will know you know.
DANA: OK. How's this? *(Gets a somber look on her face.)* I promise I will be so convincing they're gonna give me the Academy Award for best performance of the year. I'm gonna be so surprised when I walk in that door. No one will suspect I know a thing!

END OF SCENE

JOINING UP

2 Males/1 Female

CONNOR shocks his friends by telling them that he has decided to join the army instead of going off to college after they all finish high school.

LINDA: Connor . . . you can't be serious! Why don't you just plan to go to college like everybody else?

CONNOR: This makes more sense. I'll get better training, great pay, and later if I decide to go to college, I'll have the money to pay for it. The benefits they offer are amazing.

ROGER: *(Ominously.)* Unless of course, you die . . .

CONNOR: I'm not gonna die.

LINDA: Don't even joke about that.

ROGER: I'm not joking. I'm very serious. You're joining the army to "be all that you can be . . ." but what happens if they send you to war? Look what's going on in the world, man. Death *is* possible.

CONNOR: They're not gonna send me overseas.

LINDA: Roger's right. How do you know that? It's very possible that they *will* send you to Iraq or Afghanistan or some other crazed and troubled country.

CONNOR: They said most likely I'd be stateside.

ROGER: Don't be naïve, man! They'll say anything to get you to sign up. And once they have you, that's it. You're locked in. Ya gotta do whatever they say.

CONNOR: But the perks are amazing!

LINDA: Connor, don't be stupid. The perks may not be worth it if you have to give your life.

CONNOR: You guys aren't very patriotic. Don't you want to serve your country?

ROGER: I wouldn't mind serving my country, but I'm not sure if I'd be willing to *die* for my country. I wouldn't want to live anywhere else, that's for sure. But . . . I don't know . . . this is really heavy, man. I'm not sure I could make that commitment.

CONNOR: Well, I've been thinking about doing this for a long time and I really think I'm ready to make the commitment. I'm not being stupid — or *naïve*! I know exactly what I'm doing. And I definitely want to join.

LINDA: I wish you would reconsider and apply to colleges like the rest of us. I don't want you to leave.

CONNOR: Linda, be realistic — we can't all stay together forever. We'll all be going off to different places next year anyway. It's bound to happen. We're gonna grow apart — it happens to everybody.

ROGER: I'm not going anywhere. It's a J.C. for me all the way! With my grades, that's the only choice I have.

LINDA: We don't have to split up, Connor, just because we're graduating high school. We can work at staying friends. You have to want it.

CONNOR: I'll promise to send you postcards from all the third world countries I'll get to visit.

ROGER: They don't even make postcards for third world countries.

LINDA: I don't see how you guys can take all this so lightly. It's not funny. Both of you don't seem to care very much whether we all stay friends or not.

ROGER: I care. I told you, I'm not going anywhere. I'm going to junior college and I'll probably be there for four, five years! After that — who knows? It'll be very easy for you to stay friends with me — I'll be very easy to find. Pinetree Lane . . . third house on the right!

CONNOR: Linda — don't start getting nuts over this! You'll be going off to some great big four-year university and you'll make tons of new friends and you'll forget all about your old buddies Roger and Connor. Roge will be slaving away at Mickey D's and going to junior college, and me? I'll be protecting your butt by fighting to keep freedom and democracy part of the American way of life!

LINDA: Oh brother — don't take yourself quite so seriously, OK? I don't understand why anyone would want to join the service. Maybe it's a guy thing.

CONNOR: Lots of girls join up. What do you say? Want to come with me? Keep our friendship secure by fighting together side by side?

LINDA: Hey, I'm all for keeping this friendship alive, but sorry — no! I'm not the army type.

ROGER: Me either. I'd do something really stupid, like score a goal for the opposite team.

CONNOR: It's not like playing soccer, Rog.

ROGER: Well, you know what I mean. I'd be a danger to my own people!

LINDA: So you're actually gonna go through with this? We can't talk you out of it?

CONNOR: The second I turn eighteen it's a done deal. I'm joining up!

ROGER: Wow! This is it. This is for real.

LINDA: I really hope you know what you're doing.

CONNOR: Don't worry so much Linda. It's all good. We're all going to have spectacular futures. I can feel it. *(Kiddingly.)* Except Roger of course.

ROGER: Thanks a lot buddy — I see you have a lot of confidence in my abilities. But hey — I still have the potential to be successful. Doing what, I have no idea. But check me out at our ten-year reunion. I might just surprise you. I might surprise *me*!

LINDA: Seeing each other every ten years? That makes me sad. Just don't go and get yourself killed, Connor. I'd like you to stick around awhile — even if I won't be seeing you very often. At least I know you're there.

ROGER: Don't start getting all depressed yet, Linda. We still have another year to go and I don't know about you two, but I plan to have the time of my life. Before I have to start getting serious about stuff.

CONNOR: Sounds like an excellent plan to me. Whatta ya say, Linda? You in? Ready to have some fun before we have to be "responsible"?

LINDA: Yeah. Sure. Why not? One more year of high school . . . let's make it our best! Let's ROCK ON!

CONNOR: Thatta girl! It'll be a year to remember!

END OF SCENE